Serpent in the Garden

Serpent in the Garden

Amish Sexuality in a Changing World

JAMES A. CATES

JOHNS HOPKINS UNIVERSITY PRESS
Baltimore

© 2020 Johns Hopkins University Press
All rights reserved. Published 2020
Printed in the United States of America on acid-free paper
9 8 7 6 5 4 3 2 1

Johns Hopkins University Press
2715 North Charles Street
Baltimore, Maryland 21218-4363
www.press.jhu.edu

Library of Congress Cataloging-in-Publication Data

Names: Cates, James A., 1956– author.
Title: Serpent in the garden : Amish sexuality in a changing world /
    James A. Cates.
Description: Baltimore : Johns Hopkins University Press, 2020. | Includes
    bibliographical references and index.
Identifiers: LCCN 2019052333 | ISBN 9781421438726 (hardcover) |
    ISBN 9781421438733 (ebook)
Subjects: LCSH: Amish. | Amish—Sexual behavior. | Sex—Religious
    aspects—Amish. | Homosexuality—Religious aspects—Amish. | Queer
    theory.
Classification: LCC BX8129.A5 C38 2020 | DDC 306.7088/28973—
    dc23
LC record available at https://lccn.loc.gov/2019052333

A catalog record for this book is available from the British Library.

*Special discounts are available for bulk purchases of this book. For more
information, please contact Special Sales at specialsales@press.jhu.edu.*

Johns Hopkins University Press uses environmentally friendly book
materials, including recycled text paper that is composed of at least 30
percent post-consumer waste, whenever possible.

Contents

Preface

My practice as a psychologist is broad ranging. I was providing the requisite psychotherapy prior to gender confirmation surgery (GCS) for a male-to-female transgender client. We had completed several sessions when she learned in passing that I also worked with the Amish. Breathless with excitement, she asked if I knew a young adult male from a nearby settlement. In the small world of northeastern Indiana, I did. He was a friend of several years' standing, as were his parents. Still, I could not fathom the connection between a stalwart member of the Amish church and this GCS candidate. "Oh!" said my client, "when he was in that 'Rumspringa' thing, he ran around with me and my friends. He was always so sweet about guarding the women's room when I had to pee." She pleaded with me to say "hello" when next I saw her former cohort member and share her fond reminisces.[1] Part curious, part teasing, on next meeting this young man, recently chosen as a deacon in his church, I conveyed the greeting. Stricken, he begged me not to remind him of those wild, youthful days now gone. After all, they were a sinful time, and one he preferred to forget.

To make an immediate clarification, the Amish man in this vignette took Rumspringa much farther than most of their youth, roving for several years with non-Amish young adult friends who made decidedly "untame" choices. Still, this story demonstrates the difficulty of placing sexuality—anyone's sexuality—into neatly labeled categories. Imagining this pillar of the church cruising an IHOP restaurant at 3 a.m. with a group that included a transgender female was difficult enough. Picturing this same clergy member zealously guarding the women's restroom for that gender-defiant pioneer was a scene I could barely conjure.

While this story makes a point in dramatic fashion, it also demonstrates the Amish emphasis on fleeing the clutches of the world. The (now) deacon's contrition and his desire to leave the past behind was a genuine renunciation, not only of a time in his life, but also of the morals and values that time encompassed. For no person—and, exponentially amplified, for no group—is sexuality ever a simple proposition. The Amish are no exception.

The above story speaks to the essential rules, or *Ordnung*, of Amish life that control behaviors, including those in the sexual realm. Because of these stringent expectations, sexual identity and gender roles are narrowly defined. Sex and its manifestations, if featured in any role that does not involve a wife and husband, are out of bounds. For many, procreation is the purest expression of sex, but for virtually all, the man acts in the dominant role as husband, while the woman assumes a submissive role as wife. Outside the realm of reproductive necessity, sexual behavior can lure the participants into a sinful indulgence in lustful desires. While the need to limit certain sexual activities is universally agreed upon, there is room for compromise within the sanctioned union of marriage.

Still, the boundaries for sexual behavior are far more elastic than the boundaries for sexual identity. While the Ordnung can be an expansive instrument, it places numerous roles and their accompanying identities off limits. For example, the Amish are often described as "leaning" toward a Republican viewpoint, but few identify themselves as Republicans. They support Creationist theory and work to see it taught in their schools but balk at being categorized as Creationists. Amish males own firearms for hunting or ridding their property of intrusive birds or animals, but one can search far and wide for a card-carrying member of the National Rifle Association (NRA).[2] Even those Amish who teach in their schools (the majority are female) view their employment as a temporary post, not a vocation.[3]

What identities are acceptable? Christian. Male, predominantly white. Female, also predominantly white. American/Canadian. Few others are necessary, for they drive a wedge between the individual embracing that self-view and the larger group (i.e., Amish). Such a wedge increases the danger that, at least in part, the members of a collective society will fragment and find a separate or individualized sense of self (e.g., as a member of the NRA or the Republican Party). By limiting the opportunity to parse acceptable identities, the group retains its primary purpose and identification.[4]

Subsuming sexual identity into cultural expectations, however, is not as easily accomplished as avoiding social and political identities. Emotional and physical attraction for members of the same sex, transgender awareness, and paraphilic passions (fetishes) of all types can be culturally forbidden. These are inner struggles and desires, longings that drive an individual's behavior. They accompany a female as she dutifully does the wash, cooks the meals, and cleans the house. They linger with a male as he performs his work as a carpenter, does chores in the barn, or sits at the head of the table for the evening meal. To suppress these inner struggles and desires is much more difficult than to forego a political stance or embrace a categorical stand against evolution. Sexuality is emotional, psychological, physical, and biochemical. It is also social, cultural, and political. It is an intricate and passionate interplay of variables, beginning at the cellular level and expanding to incorporate the interpersonal system that surrounds the hapless human organism. For the Amish, as for all of us, it is ultimately the cultural aspects of sexuality that drive their distinct vision of who they are as sexual beings. Their norms are the focus of this much-needed book.

Amid the multitude of professional writings about the Amish, sexuality is proportionally underrepresented. An understanding of this Plain people has evolved and been articulated in so many areas, from the works of John Hostetler,[5] beginning in the 1940s, through the expanding community of sociologists, anthropologists, historians, theologians, and mental health professionals, among others, who have turned active inquiries in their direction. (Gender roles are addressed more than any other aspect, but their impact on sex and sexuality is only briefly acknowledged and then passed over.) A telling example of the hesitation to address sexual issues comes from Hostetler himself. One of his more poignant autobiographical reflections is a brief article titled "An Amish Beginning," which first appeared in 1992. In a 2005 revision, he added a section on the practice of bundling, or bed courtship, among the Amish, which had become a curiosity for the public at the time. His reference is merely a few paragraphs describing an innocent and bumbling interaction on one occasion, and it generates more questions than answers.[6]

This book is an attempt to create a professional perspective on Amish sexuality, since, as a culture, they are well known for their choice to defer matters of critical analysis and social interpretation to others. The present volume, unlike studies on many aspects of Amish life, does not build on extensive previous treatments, although it does draw from multiple perspectives and many years of research on the people themselves. For those of us who serve these remarkable individuals in the helping professions, and for those who wish to employ the Amish way of life as a model to better appreciate society as a whole, a more extensive understanding of this integral part of their lives cannot be denied.

A Model for Amish Sexuality

Models of sexuality abound, but one that at first appears paradoxical provides an excellent fit. In the larger culture, the queer community continues to grow. This term, formerly referencing persons who are gay, lesbian, bisexual, or transgender, now encompasses subcategories based on even more specific identities that continue to emerge (e.g., "queer crips,"[7] and genderfluid[8]). These subcategories pioneer new territories discovered and claimed in this age of sexual exploration. Each identity is predicated on recognizing, acknowledging, and embracing a sexual interest, desire, or state as a component of an individual's identity that diverges from what has been (and at last count, still is) the primary heterosexual norm. If the culture in which a new identity is immersed sufficiently disrupts this process of recognizing → acknowledging → embracing at the point of recognition and instead successfully interjects a process of identifying deviance → discomfort → rejection, then the sexual interest, desire, or state is categorized as a perversion. At that point, it is reduced to an unacceptable interest or impulse and fragmented as a desire or subculture to be extinguished. Its fate is far more likely to land in the rubbish pile of paraphilias or face a strong challenge to acceptance, not a newly embraced identity.

For example, despite the universal presence across cultures of those with a same-sex orientation, it is fair to say that there are no "gay" Amish.[9] The term is an oxymoron, in that gay implies a recognition of these interests and desires; an acknowledgement that they are a part of the sexual, emotional, and psychological self; and a willingness to embrace them as integral to one's well-being. Such a process is at odds with an Amish identity, which implies a recognition that sexuality is God-given, for the purpose of a man and a woman loving each other and creating life. Sexual orientation is (at present) the most salient example of the Amish effort to defend their moral borders, but it hardly stands alone. The Amish defend their morality against liberal encroachments—for example, as marriage declines and cohabitation increases, as casual sex is more readily accepted, and as marijuana is legalized for recreational use. By standing for traditional values, they fiercely embrace their cultural norms, perceived as being under attack by forces in the world that are tolerant, if not accepting, of sinful change. This choice to embrace traditional morals pushes the Amish further and further from trending mainstream cultural values. Their perceptions of sex, sexuality, and gender roles not only differ from, but also embody an active effort to avoid the influence of, the surrounding social order.[10]

Queer theory provides a framework in which to examine Amish perceptions. This school of thought initially seems to be the antithesis of their values. It evolved from Michel Foucault's writings,[11] and it has primarily been used as a social model to understand gays and, more broadly, sexual minorities.[12] Nonetheless, its concepts apply equally well to explain the behavior and values of any culture with sexual mores and norms that run counter to the mainstream. In the words of one renowned anthropologist, "At its simplest, queer theory is a critical inquiry into the alignments of sex, gender and desire that are

in the service of normative forms of heterosexuality, the heteronormative, that saturates the social and cultural order."[13]

Queer theory assumes that the heteronormative social order, or
morality imposed by the heterosexual majority, will arise in two ways.
One, it will emerge from the extant culture and its gender norms and
expectations for sexual behavior. Two, it will arise as a pushback to
norms perceived as a threat to that cultural order.[14] Accordingly, to
understand the boundaries the Amish build against sexual incursions
and the taboos they instill against internalized deviance, it becomes
essential to understand their role within Amish society and in the
larger culture: as Christians, as Americans, as Canadians, and as
members of any non-Amish group. Without an understanding of how
they perceive both their separation from and necessary integration
with the world that surrounds them, it is impossible to fully grasp
the twists and turns their logic takes in regard to gender roles and
sexuality. Thus the heteronormative of Amish culture encompasses
a history and a faith that infuses their social order and guides their
behavior. It also includes a need to respond to a culture surrounding
them, with which they interact, that is increasingly at odds with their
heteronormative ideal. In a paradox, the Amish adherence to traditional
sexual morality and gender roles now places them in the minority. It
is this unique vision that they defend.

The Genesis of the Book

It is never easy to defend a minority stance. Particularly when stak-
ing out the moral high ground, the plains below can be a lonely vista
indeed. In the words of an Amish friend, "We try to do our best, but
we also know just how human we are." The following pages respect
that effort to do their best but acknowledge that we all grapple with
meaningful ways to meet our most basic needs for safety and love, to
express ourselves as sexual beings, and to find a niche that gives us
security within a social order. In that quest, even on the moral high
ground there are times when immorality takes its toll.

This effort to collect data in order to understand Amish sexuality and gender roles is broadly based. It includes many years of interaction, informal interviews, and conversations with Amish confidantes, drawn primarily from Indiana, including Elkhart-LaGrange, one of the largest settlements, but also from smaller ones, and the other two largest settlements (Holmes County, Ohio; and Lancaster County, Pennsylvania). In addition, dialogues with multiple experts on Amish culture and society, extensive reading, and participation in continuing education programs and seminars amplify the knowledge that resonates in this book. No such study, however, can occur without input from the observer's perspective. As a clinical psychologist, psychological theory grounds my understanding of human behavior. As a Baptist minister's son, now more agnostic in my views, I continue to pursue the beauty of spiritual wisdom and respect the journeys of other seekers. And as a gay man in the seventh decade of my life, I experience an empathy, born of grief and triumph, for the struggles of any minority facing the heteronormative majority.

This effort to discuss Amish sexuality also addresses the reality of sexual behavior. As reviewers critiqued the manuscript for this book, it was notable that their comments occasionally turned on sensationalized vignettes and stories. The vignette that opens this preface was one target. Readers who find the stories included here titillating are encouraged to consider them outside the context of Amish culture. For example, take the opening story. In the third decade of the twenty-first century, does a vignette of a man guarding a restroom door for a transgender person appear steamy? Only when that man is Amish does the event even take on interest. Amish sexual behaviors and sexuality are universal in so many ways, and that is the point of including these stories. The case studies, however, have been disguised so the true participants cannot be identified.

The Framework of the Book

This volume is informally grouped into sections. The first serves as background, orienting readers unfamiliar with the Amish (chapter 1) or with queer theory (chapter 2). Amish roots profoundly influence their present lives. In an era in which all eyes look to the future, they view the past with a reverence that dictates their lifestyle choices.[15] The first chapter is a succinct overview of Amish history and their social architecture. As queer theory does not immediately lend itself to this Christian group, the second chapter reviews the historical antecedents of this model and demonstrates its application to the Amish.

The next section explores sexual behavior and gender roles. Information on sex is disseminated with an understanding that its primary purpose is procreation (chapter 3). The heteronormative of a collective, high-context culture incorporates expectations and discipline to ensure that members remain in compliance with the rules that govern behavior, the focus of chapter 4. Gender roles are an essential aspect of these expectations, as discussed in chapter 5.

Any discussion of sex and sexuality becomes emotionally detached if it does not include expressions of intimacy. This is the area where Amish culture deviates most markedly from the mainstream, since intimacy in the collective is a different experience of interpersonal sharing. The third section (chapter 6) explores this unique bond.

The final section examines sexual issues that are the most difficult to counter, since they emerge within the individual and, therefore, exist deep within the culture. The Amish do not condone the sexual abuse of children but remain reluctant to allow those who perpetrate this violation to be disciplined outside their authority (chapter 7). Paraphilic behaviors are also considered to be outside the heteronormative boundary, but those that can be successfully hidden can create an area of personal identity. This is the focus of chapter 8. Chapter 9 addresses sexual minorities, the greatest perceived threat to the Amish social order.

Whether facing the heaven-bound hopefulness of a godly life or a hell-bound descent into licentious desires, sexuality is a nagging concern for the Amish. With an approach ranging from humor to pathos, this book explores their response.

Acknowledgments

Writing is a lonely occupation. Words become an author's companion. Even when others critique, edit, or proof a manuscript, incorporating their suggestions remains a solitary pursuit. None of which changes the team effort an academic book requires. To ready this text for the publisher took an investment from many persons. And I will not name a single one.

There is a good reason for keeping anonymous those to whom I am indebted. Writing about Amish sexuality crosses a line. While my admiration and respect for these Plain people has only deepened, some will see this work as unnecessary. Worldly. Even offensive. Spotlighting an aspect of their lives better left in shadow. I disagree, or the book would not be in your hands. Ultimately, the responsibility for its existence is mine alone. To thank those who were invaluable in generating the worth these pages hold would mean much to me, but it could tarnish innocent reputations. Accordingly, I choose to omit their names.

That caveat aside, as you read, please be aware that there are unsung women, men, and even a nonbinary soul or two who were essential in creating these pages. I am so grateful for their input. Some stood by me not just on this project, but also in moments past when my bull-in-a-china-shop approach imperiled future work with the Amish. All who aided in this task and offered their support were a beacon in the darkness, much more so than they will ever know.

Two acknowledgments I can offer, the first to a place. My thanks once again to Saugatuck, Michigan. I find that former artist's colony to be a writer's mecca. And second, to the Amish who have opened their homes and their hearts, bless you. You enhance my world and enrich my life. I will be forever grateful for all that you share.

Serpent in the Garden

Chapter One

The Pilgrim Journey

Amish Discipline

The prosecutor in a rural Indiana county shared his plan to arrest two lay midwives in the Amish community located there. The action was intended to send an unequivocal message. This settlement had a long tradition of prenatal and perinatal care that too often overlapped medical services. Amish midwives, unlicensed and unsupervised, were attending at even the most difficult home births. Complications and infant deaths due to risky practices were unacceptable and would no longer be tolerated.

Once the arrests occurred, I heard from the Amish themselves. Far from protecting helpless infants from at-risk procedures, they perceived decent and caring women targeted by an unfair judiciary. A much-needed service was under attack. For a people who believe in an unwavering acceptance of God's will, a death at birth does not immediately speak to the incompetence of the midwife, but instead to the mysterious ways of the Almighty. The services these women performed allowed pregnancy and birth to remain shielded from the world, maintained within the safe confines of the community. Further, the need for a worldly physician attested to a lack of faith in God's care. The arrests were evidence of a failure to understand Amish beliefs, if not outright harassment.

These opposing views were unyielding. The prosecutor held firm in his moral and legal duty to protect the most innocent citizens of the county. A large segment of the Amish population perceived persecution by a worldview that neither understood nor cared to understand them.

At sentencing, the courtroom literally overflowed with Plain people. The defendants and their supporters were relieved when a compromise was reached. Jail time was averted, and the accused were sentenced instead to probation, with the understanding that their days of midwifery were over.

The events described above unfolded in 2018.[1] Although it is recent history, this quiet determination, a stubborn nonresistance that nevertheless finds a way to dig in its heels, is a hallmark of Amish culture.[2] It helps mold their spiritual views, their social cohesion, and the strength of their formal and informal rules. Two other Amish values play out in quiet eloquence in this vignette. Adherence to group norms supersedes the importance of the individual, a hallmark of a collective culture. And expectations of the kingdom of God supersede any expectations the statesmanship of the world may impose. These fundamental values remain virtually unchanged across five hundred years, from the Anabaptist foreparents of the Amish church to the present.

The vignette that opens this chapter exemplifies a scenario that plays out time and again with the Amish.[3] Their spiritual views, woven into the fabric of their culture, become issues of religious liberty in the justice system and are decided by the courts. In this example, a heteronormative view (the rules and morals guiding sexuality as established by the heterosexual majority)—the use of Amish midwives instead of licensed physicians—became an issue of religious liberty. In parallel fashion, the principle of morality can also become the domain of the courts in mainstream culture and its heteronormative. The decision by the U.S. Supreme Court on gay marriage attests to this. While the heteronormative in mainstream culture continues to expand, finding room for sexual minorities and what was once considered deviant behavior, the Amish heteronormative attempts to remain constrained, holding traditional boundaries. These diverging directions mark the fundamental difference in the two cultures.

This chapter outlines the historical roots of the Anabaptists, who gave rise to the Amish; reviews distinctive attributes of Amish society; and describes their social architecture.

The Emerging Amish Church

"Amish" is an umbrella term that identifies Christians numbering approximately 330,000,[4] with multiple affiliations.[5] The Amish branched from the Mennonites and trace their roots to the Anabaptist ("rebaptizer") movement. That religious impetus emerged in South Germany and Switzerland in 1525 as a part of the Protestant Reformation, a rebellion against the Catholic church. It began as a trickle, increased to a stream, and soon roared into a flood of opposition. Prominent branches included Anglicans, Lutherans, Calvinists, and Anabaptists. Pitted against an unwavering traditional theology, restless dissenters coalesced into groups who rallied around doctrinal differences that informed and influenced their cause. The willingness to die before yielding to the ultimate civil and papal authorities they defied is a staggering testament to the fervor and intransigence of beliefs at that time, both for victims and persecutors. The passionate spirit of these victims still lives today, as at least some of their children's children practice the spiritual journeys for which they were martyred.[6]

About 165 years after the Anabaptist movement began, Jakob Ammann, a new convert, was ordained a Mennonite elder. He left the Swiss Mennonites, arguing that church discipline was faltering. He perceived too relaxed an attitude toward separation from the world and a lax approach to the practice of certain rituals, such as the frequency of communion. He argued for a return to a stricter church discipline and insisted that church members avoid, or shun, the excommunicated in certain social interactions. Ammann garnered support for his platform of proposed reforms to purify the Mennonites, but his efforts were ultimately rejected. In 1693, he and his followers formed what is today known as the Amish church.[7]

Ammann has been described as an intractable and rigid leader.[8]

Based on his writings and known behavior, this is an apt description. Still, the church that emerged from his teachings, while hierarchical and demanding, lacks an emphasis on chastity and celibacy as ideals for its clergy, tenets that remain central to Catholicism. In its place, he adhered to the Protestant ideal of marriage, even instructing that clergy must be selected from married males. The Amish also maintain a strong, biblically based understanding of gender roles, including the submission of women as a heteronormative mandate.

The Amish and other Anabaptists endured severe persecution in the sixteenth and seventeenth centuries for what were perceived as heretical religious beliefs. Frequent migration, economic instability, and the turbulence of chronic warfare in Europe made immigration enticing. The Amish were primed to accept William Penn's offer of religious tolerance if they settled in Pennsylvania. Beginning in the 1740s and continuing until the mid-nineteenth century, Amish adherents came to North America in several waves. Their last congregation in Europe died out in 1936. Today the Amish live in approximately 550 settlements in thirty states, four Canadian provinces, Argentina, and Bolivia.[9] Nearly two-thirds claim Indiana, Pennsylvania, and Ohio as home.[10] They are one of numerous plain-dressing Anabaptist churches that practice simplicity of life and draw a clear line of separation from the world.

Whether limiting one's focus to the heteronormative or examining broader Amish society, the paradox between their lifestyle and the mainstream is so striking that it is easy to assume these choices are the cause and not the symptom of cultural disparities. Instead, virtually all of the unique aspects of Amish life that we observe are the result of problem solving and decision making designed to protect and preserve their values.[11] The remainder of this chapter examines these lifestyle choices.

In the twenty-first century, the signature symbol of Amish life for the outside observer is the use of horse-and-buggy transportation. While the Amish are willing to use motorized ground transportation as the need arises, ownership of a motorized vehicle risks the breakdown of community cohesion by allowing too much freedom to travel.[12] Another central tenet is their stance of nonresistance, more obvious in times of patriotic fervor, when the military is heavily mobilized. Other hallmarks of Amish culture include rejecting electricity from the public grid, speaking a Pennsylvania German dialect as their primary language, and wearing plain dress prescribed by the church. These practices were brought into sharper relief over the past one hundred years as reliance on advanced technology and the accompanying need for advanced education have become essential for daily life on a global scale.

The Amish church has no national bureaucracy or centralized ecclesiastical body. Instead, religious authority rests in approximately 2,500 small congregations that share a common set of beliefs. Despite this common core, daily practices vary among congregations. These practices are codified in the Ordnung, an oral tradition of guidelines for living that prescribes, among other things, the color and style of clothes, the order of worship, the use of technology, and acceptable interactions with the outside world. Although detailed expectations of an Ordnung vary by community, the basic cultural contours of Amish life—horse-drawn transportation, dialect, distinctive dress, worship in homes, and lay clergy—are similar across congregations.[13] The Ordnung also prohibits higher education, divorce, military service, the wearing of jewelry, and other specific practices and customs.

Yielding to the Ordnung is considered an imitation of Christ, who willingly submitted to God, even to the point of death. These guidelines for individual and corporate living, both those approved in members' meetings of the church and those passed down as an oral tradition, assume powerful religious validation.[14] Community expectations and peer pressure, present in any group but essential in a collective culture, nudge members who might otherwise stray to follow the communal norms. Nevertheless, there is room for individual thought, creativity, and expression inside the Amish moral order. Amish society does not exercise authoritarian control or relegate members to blind obedience.[15] There is leeway for unique choices. It

is the very fact that these are flexible boundaries that contributes to
the conflicts and limit setting in which the church routinely engages.

A Peculiar People

Amish culture and social norms reflect a set of religious beliefs
and commitments that serve as the foundation for their worldview.
Grasping how these commitments shape their perceptions is crucial
to understanding their development of gender roles, sexuality, and
sexual expression. The following are ten Amish religious beliefs that
illuminate their inner world.[16] The list is not meant to be exhaustive,
but it highlights primary aspects of their social structure.

1. *We are only pilgrims and strangers on a heavenward journey.*
The Amish frequently use these biblical terms to describe their lives.
They capture three core beliefs. First, "this world" is not their home.
Their hope lies in a timeless existence in the presence of God. The
physical sphere and its accompanying sorrows is therefore an in-
consequential moment. They are pilgrims on a journey, passersby in
a strange land. As visitors, they avoid entanglements in what those
mired in the world perceive as essential, such as material possessions
or fleeting happiness. The Amish recognize their responsibilities to
fellow pilgrims and to the environment in which they are placed, but
their ultimate answer is to God. All decisions and practices are shaped
by their view that the temporal will be exchanged for the timeless.

2. *We are a separate and a peculiar people.* Because they are tran-
sients, the Amish heed biblical admonitions to "love not the world
neither the things that are in the world," to "be not conformed to this
world," and similar New Testament teachings that advise Christians
to separate themselves from the temptations that surround them.
Perhaps no verse is as clear in this demand as Peter's call: "But ye are
a chosen generation, a royal priesthood, an holy nation, a peculiar
people; that ye should shew forth the praises of him who hath called
you out of darkness into his marvelous light" (1 Peter 2:9, KJV).[17]
The Amish see themselves as a "peculiar people" who have been
called out of the "darkness" of this world. While the nature of their

peculiarity is open to interpretation, they fundamentally agree that theirs is a unique Christian ministry in a sinful and even evil world.

3. *God is omniscient, omnipotent, and omnipresent. His eye is quite literally on the sparrow.* What others might interpret as fatalism is, in the mind of a devout church member, an unshakeable faith in the infallible wisdom and unfailing presence of God. His paternal, guiding hand in all that happens in human lives transcends understanding. Therefore, whatever occurs is his will and must be accepted as such. This acceptance extends to church hierarchy and discipline, as church leaders are ordained as God leads them to this calling, and the discipline of the church is his expectation. Sin, including sexual sin, is seen by God and disciplined by his ordained leaders. The heteronormative is therefore spiritual as well as cultural.

4. *To be humble is to model one's life after Jesus.* His life, as recorded in the Gospels and the Acts of the Apostles, was one of material modesty, personal deference, and an emphasis on the welfare of others. The Amish strive to attain this humility in their daily lives. It is also a requirement for a well-functioning collective culture. Expressions of pride and separate identities threaten the harmony of the church and the community. Their emphasis on accepting prescribed roles and boundaries preserves order and ensures an understanding of one's purpose within the larger group.

5. *An assurance of salvation is pride. At best, one can hope for an eternity with God.* The Amish believe in Jesus as their savior and "*hope* for an eternity with God," but they do not assert the *assurance* of salvation, as do many Christians. The reluctance of the Amish to assume the certainty of salvation reflects deep humility, expressing instead their desire that God will be a kind and merciful judge. For the same reason, they downplay conspicuous evangelism. The end result of evangelistic fervor is a vocal witness that the individual is the recipient of salvation. Such expression encourages a personal spiritual identity that wreaks havoc for a culture in which individual will is subjugated to the collective whole. For the Amish, the heavenward path demands daily efforts to follow the ways of Jesus and a

willingness to yield to wisdom provided by the elders, handed down over generations. Both that effort and that wisdom are collective in nature.

6. *Amish practice adult believer's baptism.* Beginning at age sixteen, young adults (as they are then defined) must begin to decide if they will join the Amish. Approximately 85 percent do so.[18] Baptism is the symbolic entry into the church and requires not only a confession of faith, but also a humble promise, on bended knee, to support and comply with the Ordnung so long as physical life endures. Prior to baptism, young people enter a period of Rumspringa, or running around, when they are free to socialize with their friends without direct parental supervision. Rumspringa can be one of the most misunderstood phases of Amish development.[19] Rarely do adolescents sever family ties. Instead, the vast majority continue to live at home, socialize, and work within the community. During this liminal period, they are given greater freedom from the rules that have been in place since childhood. As the months pass, however, pressure mounts for them to make a decision about church membership. If they do not join in a timely manner,[20] the normal course is to leave the family and begin life anew, separating from the culture in which they were raised.

7. *Significant sins require public confession.* Confession can be voluntary, a decision to make a public declaration of a personal struggle or guilt-producing behavior that plagues the individual. Confession can also be required by the clergy in response to sins uncovered by another. Depending on the nature and severity of the sin, the person confessing may stand, sit, or kneel (the latter for more severe transgressions) in front of the assembled church members. The nature of the sin may be shared with all the members or reserved for the clergy alone, again depending on the severity and nature of the transgression.

8. *Church discipline can involve excommunication and shunning.* In cases where a member is not sufficiently contrite, refuses to confess, or has committed a particularly grievous sin, the church can choose to excommunicate that person. The Ordnung requires that an excommunicated member be shunned, as a reminder of the broken baptismal

vow to God and the community. The ideal outcome of shunning is a spirit of wounded love, restoring the fallen one to membership. Typically, shunning involves shaming rituals of withdrawal. These can include the shunned member eating at a separate table and from separate dishes for meals, or community members refusing to engage in economic transactions with the excommunicant. Still, shunning does not fully eliminate social interactions. The degree and severity varies by church affiliation, settlement, and attitudes of the extended family.

9. *Closed communion is celebrated in spring and fall.* Members of the *Gmay* (usually twenty-five to thirty-five families comprising the local church district)[21] must be in harmony before the church proceeds with communion. Church members seek each other out to resolve differences and ask forgiveness for any slights. Gmays may handle unresolved conflict in several ways. Often, informal resolution is the first remedy. If an informal approach is ineffective, clergy can serve as mediators to resolve the impasse and engender a spirit of harmony. Some churches, however, will delay communion, at times for several months, rather than move forward in a spirit of discord. Communion is a powerful symbolic sacrament that unites the members in their commitment to each other, to the church, and to the way of life all vow to fulfill.[22]

10. *The Amish are a patriarchal society.* Bishops, ministers, and deacons hold authority within the local congregation in which they reside, and husbands/fathers hold authority within the family, while remaining subordinate to the church hierarchy. Older male siblings hold authority over younger siblings. Clergy hold the greatest authority when they meet in settlement-wide groups and coordinate their decisions, either with senior bishops or those with the longest tenure, who thus hold the greatest authority. But such meetings are infrequent and, for most decisions, leadership is localized. Unlike traditions of other churches, in which a bishop presides over a large geographic area and dozens of congregations or parishes, an Amish bishop normally oversees one local congregation. The manner in which the bishop's authority is exercised varies between and within Amish groups and by personality and disposition. While all bishops hold significant

power, they are subject to discipline as well.[23] Women vote in church business meetings and nominate men for ordination, but they are not permitted to hold clerical roles. This gender submission is a fixed aspect of Amish culture.

Social Architecture

The development of the heteronormative within Amish communities is based on a tightly defined social structure. This structure serves a practical and spiritual purpose, delineating settlements and their occupants as distinct from the world that surrounds them. Occupants are reinforced in their roles in a collective society (a practical purpose) and reminded of their unique Christian role (a spiritual purpose). The following aspects of Amish society serve as the framework that supports this structure.

Gmay

As with most social groups, the fundamental unit is the nuclear family. Unlike many Americans and Canadians in the postmodern age, however, in addition to parents who marry for life, this will include an average of five to eight children.[24] Further, in a collective culture, close bonds link adult siblings, parents, grandparents, aunts, uncles, and cousins, making extended kin key components of the social network. A middle-aged married person may have 250 people, including aunts, uncles, first cousins, and in-laws, in their primary family circle.[25] The Gmay, or church district, composes a third concentric circle in the social network. Households are in close geographic proximity. They gather for worship every other Sunday in homes, shops, barns, or basements, as services rotate between member families throughout the year. A Gmay typically consists of 75 to 150 children and adults, often including relatives. When a congregation grows too large to meet in a single home, it divides amicably along new geographic lines.[26]

Clergy

A congregation normally has a complement of four clergy—that is, a hierarchy of a bishop, two ministers, and a deacon. The bishop leads the congregation and administers rituals such as baptisms, weddings, and funerals, as well as oversees disciplinary actions, such as confession and excommunication. The deacon attends to members' financial needs related to health care, disability, and fire or storm damage to property. Each clergyman is chosen in a traditional manner, by drawing lots from a pool of nominees. Both men and women nominate married men of good standing as candidates, and candidates with the largest number of votes proceed to the final nominations. Each nominee selects a hymnal holding a hidden slip of paper. The candidate who selects a book containing a marked slip is immediately ordained. This powerful, emotional ritual, transacted in about ninety minutes, invokes the belief that God guides the ordination of the next servant for the ministry. The process eliminates the politics associated with campaigning and grants the new clergy member divine legitimacy as he assumes his tasks.[27]

Religious Services

No ritual of heritage and identity has been as resistant to change as worship.[28] Each church holds a three-hour service biweekly. This allows members to visit with family and friends in other churches on alternate Sundays. The ritual consists of hymns, a short and a long sermon, a communal meal, and visits after the service. The *Ausbund*, a hymnal first printed in 1564, contains only lyrics, as the tunes have been passed down orally across the generations. Except for occasional "English" guests (the Amish term for non-Amish) and the elderly or disabled, who may be provided with chairs, all sit on backless benches, separated by gender. Periodic member meetings are held after the worship services to consider administrative, disciplinary, or other issues that require the consensus of the congregation.

Affiliations

Beyond the local Gmay, geographic clusters of like-minded churches create an affiliation, or settlement, with distinctive practices. Point of ancestral origin in Europe, time, and emerging personalities of the leadership groups combine to create subtle and occasionally striking differences between Amish affiliations. These include Old Order, New Order, Andy Weaver, Troyer, and Swartzentrubers, to name but a few, although Old Order Amish remain the largest affiliation.[29] The affiliations within the Amish world diverge in their degree of cultural separation, social isolation, use of technology, cooperation with government, and traditionalism. Based on their degree of separation from the world and the degree of willingness to embrace technology, they create a continuum of Amish communities, anchored at one end by the most traditional. The latter can be identified by extreme limits on the use of advanced technology, stark dress, and simple homes. The most progressive groups form the opposite end. While still far distant from the technological sophistication of the postmodern or even modern era, or of current fashion, they are more apt to accommodate existing technology to traditional needs, relax expectations for clothing, and allow greater decoration in their homes.[30] Thus, for example, the most traditional groups dress in black or shades of gray, with white shirts for the men, and hand pump water, while the most progressive groups allow subdued pastel colors of clothing and permit simple washing machines.

Render unto Caesar

The importance of civil government in the lives of the Amish pales in comparison with the primacy of the church. Hence there is less need to understand municipal, state, and federal regulations and laws that the non-Amish appreciate.[31] This does not mean that Amish lay leaders and clergy who interface with the world are naïve about these expectations. It does mean, however, that these powers are diminished in their personal and corporate lives.

The phrase "render unto Caesar" pointedly underlies the sharp distinction between the dual authorities of state and church. It is taken from Christ's words: "Render therefore unto Caesar the things which are Caesar's; and unto God the things that are God's" (Matthew 22:21, KJV). While the Amish respect the "things which are Caesar's" and pray for government officials, their loyalties unequivocally lie beyond the temporal. This quiet but emphatic separation of church and state harks back to the sixteenth century, when their ancestors made the (then) heretical claim that the church should remain free from state control. Today, most Amish still decline government subsidies, whether for social services, agricultural support, or government-sponsored conservation efforts.

This disparate view of church and state is the lynchpin in the two-kingdom theology of Amish faith.[32] Allegiance to the kingdom of God is primary. Although nations, states, and even cities and towns are principalities that exist at the will of the Almighty, in Amish eyes these secular powers claim only a secondary allegiance. At the same time, government, however corrupt or undeserving, is a part of God's masterwork and is accorded respect as a legitimate power in this omniscient, albeit mysterious, divine plan. Still, conflict arises when Caesar's demands run contrary to God's will. For example, the Amish believe in the need for a basic education.[33] In the 1960s, the educational landscape in America began to transform as small rural schools were consolidated. Amish parents were concerned about the negative influence of large, impersonal institutions on their impressionable youth. As improved and advanced education became the goal of the American academic system, the Amish offered quiet resistance by removing their children from these schools.[34] The decision of several fathers to violate compulsory school attendance laws resulted in the appeal of *Wisconsin v. Yoder et al.* to the U.S. Supreme Court. In 1972, the Court ruled that the Amish maintained a religious liberty for their children's formal education to terminate at the eighth grade.[35]

In twenty-first-century America, the Amish pay their full bill of taxes: income, real estate, estate, sales, and school, with the latter a tax for a service that many do not use. In 1965, the U.S. Congress exempted Amish from Social Security (neither paying into nor receiving benefits) on religious grounds. The Amish assume a Christian duty to provide financial care for members in need and, thus, the large majority rejects both commercial and state-provided insurance.

The Amish rarely vote, although there is a minority who embrace this right. They are not allowed to hold public office or participate in political campaigns. Members of progressive Amish settlements engage in civic activities. For example, they may donate blood and can act as volunteer firemen or emergency medical responders.

The unique Amish view of the state clarifies what may appear at times to be irrational resistance as they interact with human-service agencies. For example, the state mandate for slow-moving–vehicle signs was a contentious ruling in many settlements before the owners agreed to place fluorescent triangles on their dark-colored buggies. Now some also utilize lights and blinkers.[36] Other Amish groups challenge building codes that require electrical wiring, smoke detectors, autopsies following accidents, the need to collect horse droppings, or a mandatory distance from homes for outhouses. Such discontent plays out idiosyncratically on a settlement-by-settlement basis, but these challenges reflect a deep distrust of externally mandated changes from a way of life that is their commitment to God's will.

Why would the Amish resist obvious and pragmatic safety measures? For example, who would want to place an outhouse too close to a residence? Their resistance typically involves two factors: the demand to implement worldly policies that fail to consider Amish sensibilities, and the folly of trusting human ingenuity over God for protection. The sharp doctrinal edge of the latter complaint can cut in surprising places, as the vignette opening this chapter demonstrates. Many health and safety standards that the cultural mainstream takes for granted are seen as a lack of trust in God's care or an effort to avoid the inevitable nature of his will. For the world, this view is one of irrational risk. For the Amish, it is a faith-based logic and a response to demands that gradually encroach on their beliefs and culture. The paradoxical problems they face were highlighted in a recent situation confronting two Amish men in an Indiana settlement. Ticketed for riding in a vehicle without seatbelts, they were required to confess in church, due to their failure to follow the law. When asked whether they now intended to wear seatbelts, both responded "No." They believed that wearing a seatbelt demonstrated a lack of faith in God's care.

The Amish are enjoined not to use power, force, or litigation. Still, they have empowered themselves by creating the National Steering Committee, a network of lay lobbyists and mediators who negotiate with government to resolve a host of policy and legal issues and safeguard the group's interests.[37] Nonetheless, the committee only rarely uses legal coercion to protect or advocate Amish positions. A common thread running through the causes that the National Steering Committee chooses to address is the Amish view that the state, though ordained by God, can abuse its power.[38] Those who represent the state, either directly as employees or indirectly as recipients of its support, will be suspect until they prove themselves worthy. And even when trusted, their power and authority will be secondary in purpose and vision to God's calling, that essential guide for all decisions.

Navigating Social Change

Despite the lingering myth to the contrary, the Amish are not nineteenth-century relics in a cultural museum. Their world is dynamic and evolving. The rumpled progression of social change sometimes creates cultural creases that seem silly or inconsistent to outsiders but fall into a reasonable logic within the Amish world.

Efforts by members to maneuver around regulations or laws that discourage a particular action, either implicitly or explicitly, are more often passive-aggressive or passive-resistive than open opposition, consistent with their emphasis on nonresistance. In the opening vignette of this chapter, Amish midwives practiced their profession in what was seen as a dangerous manner by English professionals. In contrast, the Amish viewed them as offering a valuable service. The outcome of the decision to prosecute two midwives was the suspension of *their* work, but other Amish midwives in the community continue to practice.

In another example, Amish teaching forbids the use of icons, an interpretation of the prohibition against graven images in the Ten

Commandments. Their longstanding conviction against posing for photographs has been tested by heightened national security and the increased demand for photo identification. More-conservative Amish groups, those utilizing the least technology, generally forbid their members to be photographed even for government-sanctioned purposes. Progressive Amish groups, employing or tolerating more technology, may not object to identification photographs but still resist videos and photographs of members by tourists or for commercial purposes.

Efforts to resist the Ordnung coming from within the settlement itself create a different problem. Passive-resistive behavior by members can be observed as churches address the onslaught of computers and online services increasingly necessary for business operations. There are efforts to balance the expectations of the Ordnung with accommodations essential to compete in a technologically savvy environment. Members may be allowed to lease or rent sophisticated equipment, or to keep such equipment in a rented space away from the home property, a rough parallel to the compromise that allows members to hire motor vehicles and their drivers but not own or drive them.[39]

Signs and Symbols

Outsiders are attuned to the most obvious aspects of Amish life: plain garb and horse-drawn buggies. Obvious differences are easy to recognize, such as the types of buggies used by the various affiliations. With only a bit more knowledge and a smidgen more scrutiny, distinctions in head coverings for women, hats for men, and other clothing styles become noticeable, too. For the Amish, however, some distinctions are even more subtle. The choice of pastel colors in men's shirts, the colors of women's dresses and the way they are pinned, the style of shoes—even the width of a hat brim—provide clues about a person's tribe and compliance with the Ordnung.[40] These markers would be trivial and unimportant in mainstream culture, accustomed to the whims of fashion. For the Amish these symbols have longstanding meaning. The appearance of homes, barns, yards, and farm equipment all have certain expectations for the decor, style, and technology that keep them within the bounds of propriety for a peculiar people. A young person's buggy may come equipped with a battery-powered, state-of-the-art sound system, but that does not obviate the remaining standards for the roof (or lack thereof), doors, wheels, springs, harness, and traces. Dress, grooming, transportation, house, yard—in a collective culture, each of these is a statement of identity, tying the owner to a specific affiliation.

On a day-to-day basis, then, these symbols reinforce the cohesion of a collective culture. In a society that defines its separation by modifying or even negating advanced technology, *absence* is as powerful a symbol as *presence*. In other words, what is missing becomes symbolically significant, be it advanced education, smoke detectors, connection to the power grid, or fashionable clothing. In contrast, symbols for us more often accentuate what is present: a Christian fish or its transition by adding feet to suggest evolution, a burned American flag, a peace symbol, a swastika, or a rainbow flag. Each evokes a strong emotional response because of its *presence*. In the absence of such symbols, we make fewer inferences about the person, dwelling, or vehicle we observe.

For the Amish, symbolic *absence* can have the same meaning. For example, in most communities a married man wears a beard, while unmarried men do not. Its absence marks one's marital status as single. In another instance, an Amish woman walked out to a van, preparing to leave for a large family gathering. Suddenly she gave a cry of dismay and ran back to the house. She had forgotten her apron and would have been ashamed to appear without it. A third case is a widow, feeling ill, who missed church. She knew, however, that her actions were suspect because of a recent quarrel with the bishop's wife. Her absence would result in a visit from the deacon. The cultural codes embedded in such symbolic messages, present or absent, offer important clues for understanding and interpreting their world.

This emphasis on interpersonal cues is evidence of a high-context culture. "High context" refers to a community with dense and overlapping relationships. Personal knowledge of others is expansive, and individuals often remain integrally involved with each other across their lifespans. Unlike mainstream society, work, play, education, family, and church life are not compartmentalized into public and private spheres. Information is more fluid, shared and considered public through this thick, interconnected web of relationships. In a high-context culture, an individual internalizes an enormous amount of data about others. Consequently, communication appears abbreviated or in shorthand form to mainstream Americans and Canadians, more familiar with a low-context culture. In low context, information is segregated into discrete social arenas, and private lives are anonymous. Because of this, far less information is globally disseminated and internalized. It is shared instead via verbal and written interactions at the point of personal contact.[41]

The heteronormative, then, as with all aspects of Amish culture, is deeply embedded. There is no need to use billboards, bumper stickers, or yard signs to announce a position on a social or political issue. A collective culture assumes such stances are known. In a high-context society, information is passed through nonverbal channels and interconnected public networks. To assume an Amish identity is to agree to the rules and behaviors of the heteronormative through attitude, group support, and signs and symbols. These rules include an intention to maintain the collective morality by supporting internal group expectations and to defend against the encroachment of external pressures to conform to worldly views.

While this overview of the Amish cannot do justice to the complexity of their culture, it does create a context for a discussion of gender roles, sexuality, and sexual behavior. Their heteronormative perception functions within these parameters.

Chapter Two

Peculiar People, Queer Theory

Many years ago, my path crossed that of a caseworker in a state agency. She was an impassioned advocate for sexually abused children, although a novice in her job. As a government employee, her primary training consisted of a meticulous understanding of the paperwork that accompanied any investigation. (This was prior to the paperless age, in which keystrokes replaced pen strokes in bureaucracies.) Her training failed to include an overview of her Amish clientele, and even had their quirks been a part of the curriculum, the behaviors she uncovered would have been considered off topic. The Amish were not yet a calling in my career, so we were mapping uncharted territory together.

She first lost her way with an Amish youth, who was about eleven years old. His case had been reported by a public-school teacher who suspected physical abuse. In completing the required interview, she found no evidence that his parents (or anyone else) had roughed up the boy, and that portion of the investigation was easily closed. Yet, in response to a standard set of questions, red-faced and sweating, he admitted performing anal sex with a male peer. Given what she *did* know about the Amish, this seemed an odd behavior. She contacted the parents of the other lad and obtained permission to interview this ersatz partner. The friend, also deeply ashamed, confessed and implicated still another male peer in having sexual contact. As these queries and interviews unfolded, she uncovered a trail of Amish male youths, ranging in age from ten to twelve years, who routinely engaged in anal sex or pseudosexual anal play. Logic dictated that an older adolescent

or adult originated these activities. Still, while her search netted about
a dozen early adolescents, she was unable to identify a penultimate
assailant. Her seasoned and more cynical supervisors eventually advised
this caseworker to expend her investigative energies in more profitable
pursuits, but she remained frustrated that a malignant perpetrator was
eluding justice. I could only commiserate.

This story nagged in my memory for years, awakening from time to
time, and leaving me to ponder its significance. Much later, working
with the Amish and beginning to address sexual abuse in the insular
communities of northeastern Indiana, I learned of the longstanding
cultural practice of "cows and bulls." Amish men now in their nine-
ties have admitted, in terse dialogue, to playing this game as young
adolescents, as has virtually every male age group from that generation down. As the caseworker in the vignette above discovered, it
consists of either actual or simulated anal sex between male peers.
This rite of passage begins at approximately ten years of age and
normally resolves itself by age thirteen or fourteen. (I discuss this in
more detail in chapter 9.)

The mysterious origins of the behavior were thus solved, but the
cultural dynamics remained a puzzle. Sexual exploration in early
adolescence seems to be a universal phenomenon. Still, the structure
and hierarchy ascribed here argues for a greater cultural molding of
these actions than is normally observed. The vehement, visceral dis-
gust for same-sex behavior that helps define mature Amish morality
is paradoxical to their cultural sanction of homoerotic acting out.
Traditional theories of burgeoning sexuality seemed inadequate to
explain this tolerance, if not its acceptance. Queer theory, a relative
newcomer among models of sexuality, offers a concise explanation.
The paragraphs below detail the nuts and bolts of queer theory. At
this point, however, its application may still seem odd. How does a
social model arising from the ostracism of sexual minorities apply to
the Amish? Several facets make it an appealing choice.

The model is elegant in the scientific sense of the word. An excellent definition of "elegance" is provided by Chris Toumey: "When a theory or model explains a phenomenon clearly, directly, and economically, we say it is elegant: one idea, easy to understand, can account for a large amount of data and answer many questions."[1] Because of its elegance, queer theory is applied by anthropologists, linguists, sociologists, psychologists, theologians, historians, those in comparative literature, and those in other fields of study. In a text such as this, which unapologetically draws from ethnography, psychology, and sociology to explain the concepts of sexuality and gender roles, queer theory is an economical and binding model.

The vast majority of applications of queer theory occur with what are, ironically, increasingly considered to be traditional sexual minorities absorbed into the queer community. Yet that does not diminish its purpose as a lens with which to focus on the response of any minority to the heteronormative. Used as such a lens, it admirably suits this book's analysis of the Amish, for they have become a sexual minority, based on their cultural and spiritual expectations.

Queer theory maintains a fixed perspective in the constructionist/essentialist debate over sexuality.[2] It argues that gender roles, sexuality, and even binary gender are socially developed, a constructionist viewpoint, as opposed to being biologically innate or genetically predetermined, an essentialist viewpoint. This argument has primarily been applied to those in the queer community, in opposition to the concept that non-heteronormative sexual interests signify a clinical disorder.[3]

Moreover, it has elegance far beyond this limited scope. Constructionism explains the interaction of power and sexuality,[4] and of religiosity and sexual minorities.[5] Its application has been argued in the development of case studies in social work,[6] and employed as a means of conceptualizing empirical research.[7] It has also been used to revisit past studies and reconceptualize their findings.[8] With regard to the Amish, queer theory applies well to a culture that encourages freedom of choice to join, but requires an ongoing commitment for acceptance, and obedience for viable participation. By virtue of the

rules governing participation in the group, the culture is constructionist by nature.

Applying Queer Theory

The underpinnings of queer theory can be found in the works of
Michel Foucault, published in English in the late 1970s and 1980s.[9]
Among other groundbreaking ideas, he argued that the "repressive
hypothesis" of sex is an example of the power that social factors play
in the expression of sexuality.[10] He believed that since the eighteenth
century, the social acceptability of sexual behaviors outside of marriage, and even of a discussion of sexuality, was suppressed. At the
same time, the freedom to openly discuss one's sexuality became an
urgent condition for personal freedom and well-being.

Foucault's arguments fueled the feminist movement, which decried
the suppression of women and encouraged their voice. His arguments
also fueled gay liberation and gave an outlet to rights for those who
found themselves attracted to the same sex. These social movements
shifted sexology from a clinical discussion into the mainstream. As
feminists and gays broadened the arena of sexuality to government,
the family, the church, and, ultimately, the media, queer theory was
born.[11] As a fundamental premise, queer theory assumes that sexuality
can be experienced, understood, and even constructed as a cultural
and historical phenomenon.[12]

For example, queer theory illuminates the dynamics behind Amish
male adolescent sex play. The cows and bulls game occurs at a developmental phase, when males experience emerging sexuality. Beyond the
mere rumblings of this physiological drive, they explore the accompanying expression of sexual power within a social context, assuming the
role of aggressive bull or submissive cow. (It would be an intriguing
longitudinal study to examine the leadership roles in the community of
males who assume dominant versus subservient roles in these games.)
The physiological drive is subjugated to situational influence—in
this case, cultural expectations. This creates a situational sexual orientation (at least situational for most). A same-sex outlet in early

adolescence thus becomes much more than basic experimentation. It becomes a rehearsal for power and control within relationships. It models the hierarchy of social roles. It gives permission for an early adolescent defiance of the cultural norms and creates a sense of self separate from the expectations of the dominant collective society. Paradoxically, it also subordinates the self to a dynamic within the group. This function—creating a unique sense of self while simultaneously subjugating that identity to the group—is essential to the well-being of a collective culture. Because these experiences are developmentally constructed, they are a phase or a rite of passage from which the adolescent emerges into a heteronormative that includes a heterosexual orientation and moral indignation toward any same-sex attraction.

Foucault's History of Sexuality

Foucault's eventual three-volume set, *The History of Sexuality*, does not elaborate a tightly woven theory. It traces historical views of sex from the classical Greek vision of pleasure to Victorian repression (the latter an illusory effort, in his view). An essential commentary on his work is summarized in the following statement: "There is not one but many silences, and they are an integral part of the strategies that underlie and permeate discourses."[13] Foucault posits that the popular view—that sex and sexuality were historically repressed, or driven from conscious awareness—is inaccurate. The ancient Greeks and Romans perceived sex as a physical act, a pleasure unencumbered by the moral standards we assign to it today.[14] Even their vocabulary for defining sexual activity translates poorly into postmodern sensibilities. Sexual drive was commonly understood as similar to other bodily urges, akin to hunger or thirst. Engaging in sexual activity lacked moral repercussions. Only gradually, and in later historical periods, were sexual desires separated from other physical functions and given a status that included a moral component.

Attempts to avoid acknowledging this aspect of bodily functions drove them out of polite conversation but also highlighted their importance. Instead of repressing sexuality, as social norms intended, it became even more essential to one's identity. For Foucault, sexuality is a discursive production. At its best, sexual identity emerges from analytical and prolonged discussion, but it is also the product of rambling and unfocused dialogue. In all ways, he perceives it as a social and cultural phenomenon.[15] Sexuality as a product of social discourse and interaction is fundamentally a constructionist theory, which argues for its social development.

Scholars focus on Foucault's discussions of same-sex behavior, as they are central to his arguments. These explain the manner in which sexuality became inextricably entangled with social and political values.[16] He underscores the change from the word "sodomite" to "homosexual" as the character of the individual moved from the discipline of the judicial to the care of the psychological.[17] In earlier times, as morality began to be applied to sexual acts, same-sex behavior was aberrant and violated the law. As such, it fell under the prerogative of the courts. This reflected a lingering convention from a time when sex was a mere physical act. As stealing to assuage hunger was still considered to be theft, so a blatantly non-procreative act to satisfy a sexual urge remained criminal. Sexual behavior morphed to a status and prominence that separated it from other physiological activities. The burgeoning field of the mind assumed responsibility for such behavior. In contrast to a manifestation of primitive desire, sexuality became an outgrowth of emotion and thought. As this alternative view became widely accepted, sexual behavior began to be recognized as a complex phenomenon, engaging social, psychological, emotional, and physiological aspects. Expectation of sole judicial control diminished, and anticipation of intervention in the field of mental health grew.

Foucault carries his premise beyond same-sex behavior to argue, in one example, that adults have increasingly withheld a discourse on sex and sexuality from children. In doing so, they choose (by virtue of "the many silences") to exercise power over information offered to the young. He argues that for there to be repression, there must be an awareness of the facts to be withheld. Accordingly, there must be discussion, dialogue, and a general knowledge of these facts. By engaging in dialogue and an open exchange of information, a large portion of the population communicates these same aspects of sexuality that are supposedly repressed. Sexuality assumes its power when an individual or group invokes a demand for silence over where topics can be discussed, or with whom. It is the silences themselves that enforce a power differential, and this power is used to control the expression of sexuality.

In the present day, Foucault's model generalizes to other groups. At the time when he wrote, gays were the preeminent emerging vocal minority that threatened the heterosexual norm, or heteronormative. Today those who are gay, lesbian, bisexual, transgender, or gender-fluid, as well as multiple other sexual minorities, meet under the umbrella of the queer community. These minorities rebel against the silences that have kept their positions out of the mainstream and minimized their power. Indeed, in the twenty-first century it is an easier task to discuss these affiliations as queer than to attempt to parse their varied, unique, and at times fluid positions. By increasing their power as a larger block—the "queer community"—instead of as separate entities, they make silences imposed by the heteronormative more difficult to maintain.

Based on Foucault's model, sexuality serves not only as a crucial element of identity, but also a crucial element of social power for any social group. It was from this point on that the early feminist movement and gay liberation began to coalesce a theory of sexuality that directly expressed their status in the larger culture and generalizes to today's sexual minorities.

Queer Theory

Queer theory is an intuitive fit for those displaced from the heteronormative.[18] Thus, for individuals whose sexuality has (a) evolved across time, (b) changed sexual orientation, (c) changed the intensity of sexual orientation, (d) included some degree of transgender awareness, (e) included a paraphilia (fetish), (f) incorporated a struggle with the manner in which sexuality integrates with identity or a gender role, or (g) in other ways transgressed what is considered the typical sexual experience, queer theory has room at the inn.[19] Indeed, for queer theorists there is no norm: "Heterosexuality is not a thing. We speak of heterosexual culture rather than heterosexuality because that culture never has more than provisional unity."[20]

Still, despite its elegance, queer theory lacks an empirical foundation. Lending itself primarily to latent variables, it resists the hypothesis testing that would add to its merits.[21] In contrast, empirical studies continue to develop a scientifically rigorous understanding of sexuality by validating binary—and therefore more immutable and essentialist—categories of heterosexual, gay, and bisexual orientations. In doing so, they avoid the cacophony of drummers to which those adhering to queer theory march.[22] The choice of models then becomes queer theory, which is an amorphous framework, or the operational definitions of traditional theorists, which largely continue the effort to unpack binary sexual orientations. The lens of queer theory offers a perspective on sexuality that is more attuned to reality but lacks definition. Sexual orientation, identity, and gender roles are intertwined and are perceived as a function of environment, learning, and culture, with biophysiology demoted as a driving force. Because each variable—environment, learning, and culture—is in flux across one's lifespan, sexuality is in flux as well, so that identity, sexual object choice, and gender roles are permeated and influenced by external as well as internal experiences and, in turn, influence the entire range of social behavior and self-awareness. This model also combines power and control as integral aspects of sexuality.[23]

Queer theory is a good fit for a social group that attempts to disenfranchise sexuality, curbing recognition of non-heterosexual, non-procreative, and unmarried identities. The more quiescent a culture becomes about sex, the more it must covertly dialogue about those aspects it chooses to withhold. Repression requires discussion. "Queering" these actions, a term for deconstruction of the process, is necessary to understand these dynamics.[24] This book is an attempt to queer a traditional Christian collective culture for whom sexuality is integrated in complex and sophisticated ways. Queer theory offers a clear and direct understanding of the overt and covert processes that are used. For the purpose of understanding the Amish, elegance trumps empiricism.

Their reluctance to verbally acknowledge sexuality is also facilitated by a high-context culture, with its reliance on visual cues and a shared history to communicate information. Gender roles remain firmly assigned. Expectations for appropriate behavior—that is, the Ordnung—are primarily unwritten, but they are still codified in such a way that the entire community is aware of them. The dissemination of power is based on gender, followed by age, so this hierarchy is pervasive in daily life. These are not values commonly expressed. Instead, they are values in which the community is steeped as a part of their collective awareness, repeatedly reinforced by high-context cues. These expectations, the discipline of Amish life as a form of learning, and the group as a collective culture mold an individual's understanding of sexuality and gender roles in the immediate moment, as well as in transition across one's lifespan.

Queer theory is also useful because of its elegance among disenfranchised groups. Although the Amish are not usually seen as disenfranchised, their choice to be separate from the world is zealously guarded and limits many rights and privileges. In so doing, the social constructs of power and control become essential considerations, for to maintain their chosen identity, they guard the borders formulated against interactions with the world and simultaneously nurture a sense of cohesion within their own communities. Sexual identity, incorporated within the larger sense of self, is maintained in this combination of boundaries and cohesion. Some degree of separation is a necessary process among any minority that acts as a unified group, and this involves the exercise of power and control.[25]

Despite its utility and elegance, queer theory may still seem at odds in its application to a staid Christian group.[26] Because queer theory emerges from the antiestablishment stances of feminism and gay liberation, it has been posited as a theory of rebellion.[27] As Arlene Stein and Ken Plummer note, "At its wildest and Wilde(st), queer theory is a plea for massive transgression of all conventional categorization and analyses—a Sadean/Nietzschean breaking of boundaries around gender/the erotic/the interpersonal, and a plea for dissidence."[28] In advocating an unconventional approach and rejecting the dualism inherent in traditional models of sexuality, queer theory argues for a fluid conceptualization. Identity is perceived as dynamic, and even transient, over the course of time.[29] In this dynamism, it does fit the Amish. There is a fluidity to sexuality and identity in their lives that is misunderstood. As the example of the game of cows and bulls demonstrates, a flexibility exists that is overlooked by more-traditional analyses.

Queer Theory and Amish Culture

The following are specific applications of queer theory to Amish culture.

1. *The purposes of discursive limitations as a form of power and control can be deconstructed.*[30] Any reader who has perused an Amish periodical, such as *Family Life* or *Young Companion*,[31] knows that sexual topics are mentioned indirectly, if at all. Such avenues are closed, lest a reader be offended. This reticence in the printed word reflects a cultural discretion for the venues in which sex and sexuality can be discussed. A frequent and surprisingly frank level of discussion, however, can occur in acceptable forums. The repressive attitude of the Amish toward sexuality means that subgroups monitor, communicate about, and implement the restrictions that maintain cultural standards. The power and control that surround the creation, utility, and management of these limitations are central to their heteronormative and are an essential component in understanding Amish sexuality.

2. *The nature and purpose of both cross-gender and within-gender roles can be deconstructed.*[32] The submission of women in a patriarchy is a given. The nuances of that submission, however, are negotiable. In reality, although the ultimate role of females is inferior to that of men,

their power varies, depending on the settlement, social status, maturity, and the dynamics of the individual family. Queer theory assumes that the creation of gender roles both predicates and is predicated on multiple influences that lead to greater or lesser power within the social hierarchy. Although gender roles are the salient force, there are further refinements in the heteronormative that dictate the manner in which males and females exert authority. While still primarily based on a hierarchy of age or maturation, the degree of identification and cohesion with the collective culture, and perceptions of willingness and an ability to fulfill the anticipated gender role, contribute to social endorsement of an individual's gender identity.[33]

3. *The role of marriage can be deconstructed as both a commitment and an identity.* In the postmodern world, the ideal may remain a lifetime commitment for married partners. Statistics paint a different picture. For the Amish, marriage remains a decision that is anticipated to exist across the couple's lifespan. As such, a husband and wife engage in more than a partnership. Their marriage, and the family ties that it creates, become a merged identity for the family members and are embraced by the collective culture. Gender identity is intertwined with the expectation of this long-term heterosexual union and the interplay of power and control within that relationship.

4. *Cultural treatment of sexual behavior defined as "deviant" can be deconstructed.* Authority can have a subtle influence on cultural mores and expectations. In contrast, it is almost always a direct influence on sexual misconduct. It facilitates emotions such as guilt, shame, regret, and remorse. It commands public confession as a means of reeling in drifting sexual identities to conform to the heteronormative. In a collective society, it places not only sexual behavior, but also the evolution and devolution of sexual behaviors, thoughts, and feelings into context. The effort to maintain cohesion, binding members by common beliefs and practices, is seldom more fraught with danger than in the expression of unacceptable sexual behaviors. Simultaneously, as the revelation of certain sexual thoughts and feelings is

repressed, acceptable venues for discussion are limited. This creates a risky subculture of members who either engage or desire to engage in a sexual acting out that defies the heteronormative.

5. *Amish perspectives on sexuality as it is practiced and portrayed outside their community can be deconstructed.* Sexual identity and efforts to manage it are not only generated by values within the culture, but also by the perceptions and values the culture struggles against. Accordingly, an understanding of Amish perceptions of and attitudes toward sexuality as it is practiced in the world demonstrate the forces aligned against their cultural heteronormative. The power wielded within the collective culture is an attempt to enact control against these influences.

The Interplay of Forces

The interplay of three systems influences the expression of sexuality in Amish culture. One, the response is dictated by tradition and by expectations or rules for living, which are defined by the Amish social system. This is the Ordnung, or rules. Two, their culture endorses heterosexuality as the preferred behavior and gives it a privileged status.[34] This norm is shared by many conservative groups. Three, the Amish also value a Christian discipleship tradition, integrating personal faith and a commitment to Christ's commands. It is this intersection of the Ordnung, heterosexuality, and spirituality that creates the Amish heteronormative. The group with which one identifies offers the strongest sense of sexual self.[35]

An emphasis on a social construction of sexual orientation, however, challenges the assumption that there can be a "normal" or "natural" path. The hypothesized fluidity of sexuality argues that an individual's orientation can and does change or evolve across one's lifespan in response to environmental circumstances.[36] (The strength of that flux, however, remains in question.) As the urgency of biological and physiological mandates is downplayed, social context, particularly social power, assumes a central role.[37] The following model uses the passage of the Amish through their lifespan to display the efficacy of this concept.

Queer Theory across the Lifespan

A child arrived just the other day
He came to the world in the usual way.[38]

The opening lyrics of this Harry Chapin folk song remind us that the miracle of birth is the same throughout the globe. For Amish infants, their world is an extended kin network that shares responsibility for this new life. That responsibility includes teaching each of them an appropriate gender role and identity. Once a child reaches the proper age, clothing will be gender appropriate, too. (In some settlements, boys are first clothed in dresses, to facilitate diaper changes.) Children will be given responsibilities that match their gender, maturity, and capabilities. If attending an Amish school, textbooks include stories that highlight the differing tasks and responsibilities of boys and girls. As a boy matures and can handle independent household chores, he becomes responsible for the animals and the farm, while a girl takes on tasks such as cooking, cleaning, washing, and sewing. Chores are interchangeable as circumstances dictate, but "his" and "her" chores remain defined as such.

Once children reach the age of sixteen, they find a group of friends with whom they can run around until they make a choice about the ultimate course of their lives. These will be peers of the same gender. Although they will visit groups of the opposite gender, males and females will not socialize together, except in larger groups, until they choose to date. As dating turns serious and a couple contemplates marriage, they will join the church, if they have not already done so, as a step in that direction. Their marriage will follow soon after.

The male assumes primary responsibility for securing living quarters and ensuring that his employment will support the couple—his role in a patriarchal society. The female is in charge of household chores and prepares to become a mother—her role as a submissive wife. Heteronormative expectations still leave room to negotiate power and control within the relationship, but as church members, the couple will adjust to the authority of the church in their lives in a much more pervasive way than was true when they were children. Again, this submission to the church is a part of the collective culture and the heteronormative, as it is practiced in Amish society. At some point a husband may be nominated for the ministry, if he is seen as a stable man who would be a good leader. If chosen as a deacon or minister, his burdens will increase as he becomes responsible for the administration of the church.

As the couple has children of their own, the cycle begins again. Parents eventually consider retirement, and often build a *dawdyhaus*, or small home, next to one of their children. There they can live out their lives in security and comfort, as they will be provided with support and care. They become members of the extended family, modeling the expectations for heteronormative behavior and reinforcing the rules as longstanding members of the collective culture.

Queer theory applies to this lifespan experience in several ways. From an early age, there is a significant pressure to limit experiences of intimacy to the confines of Amish society. An emphasis on plain dress,[39] the importance of extended family, and geographic limitations to travel all signal the importance of remaining close to home, both to create enduring relationships and to reinforce cultural control. A young man is groomed from an early age to assume the authority and responsibilities given to males, just as his female counterpart is groomed to assume her complementary role. Expectations for behavior and interactions are predicated on firm gender roles from birth forward. These shift and accommodate the cross-section of maturation and circumstances across one's lifespan, but they remain in step longitudinally with social demands.

Acceptable sexual intimacy is limited to the opposite sex, and here controls over involvement are strictly enforced. Rumspringa behavior between genders is monitored as much as possible as the intimacy of childhood with same-sex peers gives way to opposite-sex dalliances. In maintaining control through these social rituals, the power of sexuality is contained and managed, so any sexual behavior that does occur outside of strictly established parameters is considered to be acting out, a social taboo for which all parties will experience shame and guilt. Only after marriage is sexual behavior condoned, reinforcing the control and, hence, the power of traditional expectations.

If a man is chosen for the ministry, the authority of the male role is enhanced as he dons the mantle of clerical responsibility. This is a transition that accrues only after he has met the appropriate steps of church membership, marriage, and demonstrable maturity. His power has been expanded by his accession to this status.

The importance of the family is reinforced as parents age. They are now in the care of their children, through the institution of the dawdyhaus. Again, power and control accrue to the traditional family and are a reminder that the gender role of provider continues to shift and change across the course of a lifespan for both the elderly and the children who provide for them.

Throughout the life cycle, however, the hierarchy of power in Amish culture remains the same. Power is generated from a spiritual as opposed to a temporal source. The triune and masculine God (Father, Son, and Holy Ghost) is the seat of all authority, as revealed in scriptures. God is autocratic, and his rule is the iron will of a king. The structure of government within this kingdom aligns with the bureaucratic necessity of earthly kings. The church serves to geographically divide an unwieldy number of subjects into manageable units, while the clergy, although chosen by consent of the governed, serve at God's will.

Intermediate to scripture and church is the Ordnung, the rules that proscribe and prescribe the routines and behaviors of daily life. These rules both emerge from the culture and, as they are examined and modified, serve as a weather vane for the direction in which the culture is moving. In the context of power and control, the role of the church and its guardians—the clergy—is to ensure that the Amish ship of state hoves close to the shoreline of scriptural injunctions, guided by these rules.

Below these sources of power is the family. Although it is the foundational building block for temporal organization, in a collective culture the family, as a unit, does not function independently. It melds into the identity of the larger group. The dynamics of power and control within the family mirror the patriarchal hierarchy in the larger social structure, with the father as the head of the family system. The mother assumes a substantial role, but one that is subservient to the father, and children have a deferential role to any adult. Behind the social façade, families engage in a much more fluid system of cooperation, consultation, shared authority, and, at times, matriarchal dominance. Ironically, this discursive component is necessary to maintain the external heteronormative structure, for it allows dialogue and modifications that maintain the desired status quo as the family interacts with the broader cultural network.

This wide-reaching understanding of queer theory applies to the entire social fabric of Amish life. It reflects the integration of gender roles into the social construction, welfare, and status of their environment, learning, and culture. But what of sexuality, specifically?

Amish Sexuality

The nomenclature "Plain people" may imply that their sexual behavior is easily understood, but nothing could be further from the truth. The Amish separate themselves from the world, but they cannot divorce themselves from their sexual desires, nor from the complex demands that sexuality creates. For example, one author mentions an Amish couple who were accepted and much beloved by their community. The fact that the wife was intersex, with nonfunctioning male genitalia, was either overlooked or quietly accepted by both her husband and the community in which she lived, despite the fact it would have been common knowledge in a collective culture.[40] Likewise, I was once approached and asked to explain the death of an Amish young man, based on an obtuse coroner's report. As I read the document, it became clear that he had died accidentally, cross-dressed, while practicing autoerotic asphyxiation.

The complexities of Amish sexuality were driven home with even greater force as I worked with a group of Amish men who wanted to create a booklet to support those who struggled with sexual sin. The members included one man who had overcome compulsive masturbation, and a second man with a history as a voyeur. A third had been sexually abused as a young child and believed he had resolved that experience until his son was born. The child's presence stirred shameful memories that he had long forgotten. Sexual identity for these men was shaped by the power of the culture in which they lived. It denied them a voice for experiences that fell beyond acceptable boundaries; the repressive hypothesis at work! They could share such information freely with an English counselor, as well as with each other in his presence, but they did not feel that same level of freedom in their own communities. The Amish heteronormative rejected such overt acknowledgment of their experiences.

The limitations these men confronted were best expressed by a humorous story shared by one participant. He told of a widower in his church who remarried when well into his sixties. His bride-to-be, also widowed, was close in age. During a conversation with a group of men, a fellow church member teasingly asked the groom about his intentions toward sexual relations, since the only legitimate purpose for sex was procreation. His shopworn (purported) response? "We may be too old for children, but we're never too old for miracles. We're going to try!" The story emphasizes the need to remain within the expectations for sexual behavior, even when these expectations were patently unattainable. The power of this prohibition was diluted, as all present were aware that the man's identity included a healthy appreciation for his desires. Yet the story, apocryphal or otherwise, demonstrated a means to avoid a direct confrontation with the expectation that sexual behavior should occur solely for procreative purposes.

Gender roles among the Amish are likewise much more complicated than they first appear.[41] Amish society is patriarchal, with men in the roles of clergy (bishops, ministers, and deacons) and fathers at the head of the family. Women submit to men, and children submit to adults. Further, the roles for males and females are superficially binary, carefully categorized, and strictly bounded. With these limitations understood, however, women's roles are often equalized. Their power is not as often directly expressed, but it remains an influence within the home, the family, and the church. Their opinions will not be in the forefront. The male hierarchy will be present as the guiding force. But women's choices, and at times their decisions, can be an overriding factor in the background. Perhaps more so than for men, their status and their gender role change across time, as they move from being single to married, and from being employed outside the home as young women to homemakers, then parents, and, ultimately, matriarchs in large families. As their role changes, they find that their power, their perceptions of their sexual identity, and their interactions with their family, church, and community all transform. Men change as well, but, within a dominant patriarchal role, their transformations are less pronounced. Still, they transition from single to married, become eligible for the status of clergy, and can be chosen to serve on school boards. As they mature, they become patriarchs in ever-widening family circles.

The remaining consideration is the Amish response to the world that surrounds them. While they live in sheltering settlements, they are not sequestered. Any Amish person who chooses to do so has daily interactions with the world, be it through media such as newspapers or books, phone contact, personal interactions, or the simple act of observation as they go about their daily lives. They cannot help but be aware of the sexuality that plays out around them. They may choose to avoid discussing its presence, but that does not change its existence—or their awareness of it. The heteronormative in mainstream culture is a power of its own, and Amish pushback against this system strongly influences their own beliefs.

The remainder of this book explores Amish perceptions and responses to sexuality and gender roles. It also examines the reactions and behaviors of those who work with them.

Chapter Three

The Birds and the Bees
(and the Horses and the Cows)

Learning about Sexuality

I was spending time with an Amish young adult of several years' acquaintance. We knew each other well and he felt comfortable posing questions about life dilemmas. This one, however, took me by surprise. "I know how men get pleasure from sex. How do women?" My response weighed the opposing responsibilities to the two women I considered parties in this query. On the one hand was his mother. I am sure I contributed to calluses on this formidable matriarch's knees as she prayed, asking God's guidance for her impressionable son whenever he was with me, a wayward English influence. She would be thankful for my silence. On the other hand was an Amish woman I had yet to meet. I was certain that his wife, whomever she might be, would value a husband knowledgeable in how best to meet her needs as well as his.

In the years since, I have attended his wedding, played pattycake with his oldest, and continued to meet with his mom and dad. In deference to the cultural expectation that sex is not readily discussed, that question and its outcome has never been mentioned again. In this case, ignorance is indeed bliss.

Lest the Amish come off as particularly inept, a quote from *Seinfeld*, that wildly popular television comedy, reminds us that this is a universal struggle: "You know, nobody knows what to do. You just close your eyes and hope for the best."[1] The character Jerry Seinfeld offers moral support to his friend, George Costanza, as the two commiserate over the difficulty in truly knowing whether one has pleased a female sexual partner.

This vignette and the *Seinfield* quote begin a chapter on sexual awareness among the Amish as a teasing reminder that they are not alone in struggling with the mysteries of this realm. From the writings left by the ancient Greeks to postmodern sitcoms and documentaries, the endless explorations and analyses of sex do little to integrate and incorporate that knowledge into an egalitarian system in any culture. Sexual behavior often remains a set of contrasts: self-fulfillment or an expression of love, a bargaining chip or a romantic interlude, and frustration or a source of pleasure. Perhaps the universal awareness is that between the motion and the act falls the shadow,[2] which fuels our frequent discomfort discussing the mechanics of sex beyond efforts to titillate ourselves and our partners. We avoid a more sophisticated understanding, preferring to leave it shrouded in mystery.

To encourage the primary purpose of sexual behavior as procreation in no way dismisses the conflicted need to understand it. Foucault's repressive hypothesis comes directly into play with his belief that the more restrictions placed on overt discourse about sex, the more discourse occurs in alternative ways.[3] To understand the heteronormative of sexual behavior as it unfolds for the Amish is to conceptualize their perceptions of the need for knowledge, the role of pleasure, and the role of sex (as procreation) in God's plan.

Knowledge and Sexuality

The biblical allegory of the Tower of Babel (Genesis 11:1–9, KJV) has fallen into disfavor in recent years, even as a metaphor, replaced by an emphasis on complex cultural origins and multicultural parity. Still, the story is pertinent here. In brief, the people decided to build a magnificent city. Its centerpiece would be a tower that reached to the sky. Angered by their audacity, God foiled the plan by causing them to speak different languages. Baffled in communication, they could not cooperate, and the work was stymied. The story embodies a fundamental and deeply interwoven truth for the Amish. Pride is anathema to God. Any effort to emulate him is hubris. To attain knowledge beyond that needed for the tasks of everyday life is arrogance. Sexuality is included in that body of unnecessary knowledge.

The Amish strive in several ways to confine their knowledge to that required to serve God. Formal education, often utilizing a system of Amish schools, ends with the eighth grade. Within these eight years, the information a "scholar," or Amish student, acquires will be limited to fundamentals deemed necessary to negotiate basic business practices, understand the environment at a practical level, and make household and life decisions. The science proffered there includes basic principles, and Creationism is the model that explains the emergence and longevity of the universe. Health textbooks offer a rudimentary understanding of the human body but make no attempt to provide sexual education.[4] Academics complement knowledge obtained at home, but the classes are not designed to stimulate a further desire for learning, nor are they a foundation for those who aspire to higher educational goals. Self-contained and complete, they prepare the scholar to finish that eighth year with the formal training needed for a life of service to God.[5]

Learning proceeds apace in a parallel course at home, although the curriculum is different. Amish children care for animals (even the smallest farmette must still house the horses that pull buggies), tend the garden or crops if in season, and participate in the inevitable household chores, in part divvied up by gender, including cooking, sewing, laundry, cleaning, repairs, and maintenance. As is true in the school setting, knowledge gained here is self-contained and complete, a means of preparing a young person for Amish life.

This broad cultural framework incorporates their heteronormative. From formal to practical educational experiences, Amish children are reminded that they are part of a collective society. Within it, gender roles and the expectations for appropriate gender behavior are ordained by a power beyond the material world. As important as what *is* taught is what is *not*. Absence is a primary component of Amish culture (see chapter 1). There is no need for information considered to be unnecessary to live a pleasing life in the service of God. In refuting wisdom deemed essential by the world, the Amish turn their backs on mainstream views and opt for a unique vision of interpersonal, financial, and practical living.

Rarely is there an emphasis on sex education in an Amish home, but children are aware of sex from an early age. They routinely observe animals mating. And yet this rudimentary grasp of sexual activity is not amplified or expanded by prolonged discussions. At the appropriate time, mothers explain menses to daughters (or sisters to younger siblings), and more-open families describe sexual activity and pregnancy. It remains for children to incorporate their understanding of sex, garnered from peers and older siblings, with the accompanying myths and misconceptions that accrue as adolescents impart such education, along with their modifying distortions.

Even in adulthood, information about sex is minimally acknowledged. In 1781, Bishop Hans Nafziger wrote a letter explaining church discipline (i.e., doctrine and practices), which continues to be circulated.[6] Nafziger outlines the formulary for an Amish wedding service, including instructions for the couple prior to their marriage. He states, "In the counsel they [the couple being married] are told [by the ministry] that the man should not go to the wife in the time of her menstruation, but should withhold himself according to Leviticus 15."[7] Although this letter continues as a primary source of sexual advice for some, others supplement it with more-current information.

Overt displays of affection between Amish couples are rare, reinforcing the private nature of intimate physical contact. Depending on the settlement and the progressiveness of the church, an Amish woman may opt to have her first child at a hospital, under the supervision of an obstetrician/gynecologist. If that birth is uncomplicated, further pregnancies may be managed under the watchful eye of a midwife. Some are healthcare professionals licensed by the state. Others are lay midwives. In either case, gestation and birth remain shuttered within the community.[8]

The Amish emphasize a straightforward, unequivocal acceptance of the physical environment. It is created by God and acknowledged as his. Generalizing this worldview, the emphases above apply not only to sex, but also to all aspects of thought and behavior. The individual immersed in the church and this collective culture does not engage in extensive critical thinking. To ponder, to analyze, to critique, or to investigate philosophical or moral issues in depth invites the potential for a risky emotional and psychological journey away from the values and beliefs that bind the community.

The heteronormative, as applied here, involves a delicate balance. Amish culture is not so rigid that it demands an unwavering allegiance to community standards. There is room for contemplation and growth, although many aspects of sexual behavior and sexuality are held at bay. Still, curiosity and questioning occur, within limits. The Ordnung is flexible enough to allow experimentation. The church can always reaffirm or reinstate a prohibition if needed.[9]

For example, a newly married wife may begin to struggle with her relationship and experience an existential angst about her life partner. Abstract thoughts, such as the meaning of intimacy, aspects of the relationship, and the merits of her decision, lead her to question not only the marriage, but also the validity of her faith and her commitment to the Amish church. That angst is better served (in the Amish view) through a prayerful recognition that doubts signal weakness in one's faith, and that her anxiety is more usefully absolved by making concrete choices to improve her role in the marital relationship. Answers to her philosophical concerns are far beyond what is necessary for her role or station.

The cultural mandate above funnels into a logical but inaccurate conclusion: the Amish require a simplistic view of sex and sexuality. Instead, the Amish limit solutions once an issue is identified. Dissatisfied in a marriage? Options such as an open marriage, divorce, or even a temporary separation are not acceptable. In love with another person's spouse? Act on these feelings and, with discovery, the consequences are swift and sure. Instead, learn to deny them. Not ready to settle into married life? Or unwilling or unable to have children?

The community stops short of overt rejection but casts a pall over one's acceptance. For single men, the potential to join the ministry is forever closed. Historically, single women become maiden aunts, expected to provide childcare for their relatives and often perceived as unfulfilled because they lack children of their own. Procreation is an anticipated part of the life journey. (There are indications this role may be changing. Unmarried women in some settlements more frequently express their satisfaction with this state, joining together for trips and activities and defying the convention that they are marginalized because of their status.)

While options are limited and tightly controlled, adjustments to these options have a greater breadth of possibilities. It is here that the Amish demonstrate the validity of the repressive hypothesis (i.e., dialogue must occur about what is to be repressed). Return to the example of the newly married, struggling wife. The church will not condone even the thought of separation or divorce, much less a temporary respite from the church. Nonetheless, as a collective culture, the entire community will know of her struggles. This is not considered gossip, or meddling, but support, as her immediate and extended family, church members, and friends provide nurture and hope—as well as impose cultural controls—for this fledgling couple. The community is aware, at an unspoken level, of the risk for the situation to develop into a loveless marriage or, even worse, their separation. The ultimate danger is that the couple could leave the Amish church. Thus the community will make every effort to enhance the quality of the pair's relationship. But in doing so, there will not be an emphasis on abstract or existential concerns. The focus will be on fundamental, concrete ways of interacting. Intimacy and sexual gratification, if discussed directly, will be handled through discrete channels designated to address these issues. The fact that sexual activity remains largely unspoken in no way diminishes its importance in a marriage, as the community also assumes that children are necessary to complete the family.

In this way, although not a directly articulated focus, sexual behavior is predicated as essential to marriage. The heteronormative ideal in this respect includes not just sex, but reproduction. In contradiction to the mainstream, children are evidence that the consummation of the marriage has been achieved to fulfill God's plan and did not occur solely as a selfish or pleasurable act. Given this expectation, what role does pleasure play? And how is sexual pleasure integrated with the knowledge needed with regard to sexual behavior?

Gender, Pleasure, and Sexuality

The pleasure of sexual behavior is long embedded in the Christian tradition as a source of temptation. Paul, arguably the most philosophical of the New Testament writers on sex and sexuality, encouraged believers to abstain but reluctantly approved of marriage for men who could not suppress their carnal appetites (1 Corinthians 7:1–2, KJV). For him, when sex was intertwined with pleasure, base human nature emerged, separating humanity from God. Instead, the hedonistic urge should find a balance in more-worthy outlets.[10]

Once again, the fundamental Amish dilemma does not differ from the conflict that emerges for any individual, in any culture, albeit one cynically addressed by St. Paul. A primary developmental task for the egocentric infant is delayed gratification, as a first step toward empathy. The principles of cooperative interaction are the basis for communal harmony, whether in a family or a larger social group. It is the weighted values that their culture places on productive behavior (work) and leisure activity (play) that separate the Amish.

Within mainstream culture, work often involves employment outside the home. An investment in the production of goods or services for a company includes cooperative effort with others one knows from the work setting. Friendship with these persons, if it develops, emerges as a result of repeated contact in that setting. A transition from one place of employment to another means a renegotiation of relationships. Moreover, the role of employee is defined and delimited by vocational expectations. Once home, the individual assumes a different set of roles. Regardless of whether the employee emerges from a factory, office, vehicle, or some other type of job, a retreat from work includes as many labor-saving technological innovations and luxury items as finances allow. Pleasure is defined by the ability to work less for more pay and by the consumption of technological products that ease the workload at home.

In Amish settlements, males increasingly work outside the home.[11] Even so, employment remains an extension of their culture. Whether with a construction crew or on a factory floor, Amish employees are surrounded by peers who engage in similar tasks, working the same hours and living in the same epicenters. Others remain within the community, manufacturing goods or offering services that can be generated from that cradle of support. In either case, the men primarily engage in physical labor. Their wives are the homemakers. Women may supplement the family's finances by generating goods or services part time, but their essential role will be that of caring for the home and parenting. They take responsibility for cooking, cleaning, shopping, performing household chores, and supervising the children.

If a husband remains at home, he shares these responsibilities. The wife also shares chores with and finds assistance from other women, often family and extended family members, as she goes about her daily activities. If a husband works outside the home, on his return he will blend into the demands of the household. Sophisticated technology will not ease the burden of the comparatively numerous activities to be completed if the household is to run at peak efficiency. Pleasure emanates from a sense of accomplishment when the work is done, with all family members fulfilling their prescribed duties. Amish society and Pauline christianity create these heteronormative roles and their subsequent satisfactions.

Compared with Amish culture, in the mainstream, pleasure has been separated from accomplishment and made a hedonistic right. We minimize physical exertion and maximize luxury. The Amish accept a greater expenditure of energy and a comparatively stark environment. The mainstream achieves satisfaction and a sense of pride from working less and consuming more. For the Amish, these sentiments come from working harder and consuming less. In each culture, pleasure is earned and is attached to status. The Amish however, find gratification in submitting to a strong moral code, with less of an inherent right to pleasurable experiences. This carries over into the sexual realm.

The Amish derivation of pleasure is easily deconstructed by queer theory. Sexual activity carries a dual role. Its primary purpose is procreation, a doctrinal mandate. Yet it is also a pleasurable act and, as such, falls under the expectations of an earned reward, thus gaining social power. How does that social power play out?

If pleasure is reframed from a hedonistic right (in mainstream culture) to a reward for appropriate actions (in Amish culture), it becomes a privilege. To return to the admonition of St. Paul, pleasure no longer aligns with a creative opportunity for individual expression, but with a release of tension for those who lack appropriate self-control. Ideally, then, pleasure in sexual behavior for the Amish emerges as satisfaction in having been a faithful spouse and a conscientious Christian. It is inextricably connected to the act of procreation and to the joy of living an appropriate lifestyle. Even the physiological enjoyment of sex is harnessed to the purpose of sexual behavior in their overarching heteronormative cultural standard, which is the topic of the next section.

Procreation and Sexuality

There is no edict at once so straightforward and complex as the biblical command to "be fruitful, and multiply" (Genesis 1:28, KJV). Building on this early verse, injunction after injunction, from both Hebraic and Christian traditions, explain just how that multiplication should occur and what the behaviors are that violate its intended purpose. The Amish tradition resists the fiercely contested thoughts these traditions engender. For them, there is a primary purpose for sexual behavior, and that is procreation.

But if there are other purposes for sexual behavior than procreation, then what? As the story told by the Amish man in the previous chapter suggests, the need for sex being solely for procreation is accepted with a wink and a nod. Still, a willingness to allow one poor soul with a sob story through the turnstile does not mean that such access is now free for everyone. Penile penetration of the vagina in a marital relationship remains the undisputed acceptable sexual act. For the Amish, this is the natural, intended, God-given sexual purpose for genitalia. All others risk being categorized as deviant and sinful. That injunction has led to many a confession to the assembled church. Imagine a sexual behavior and it probably has been confessed there. Forms of sexual activity outside of vaginal penetration for the purpose of procreation fall within the category of deviance in at least some settlements, and thus are considered sinful.

The expectation of sexual behavior serving the primary purpose of procreation is a powerful social control. It is impossible to meet this rigid standard, perhaps with the exception of persons disciplined to the point of exhibiting a clinical syndrome. For example, an Amish wife who cannot achieve orgasm through intercourse could be denied this pleasure. A couple who participates in any type of foreplay that results in a climax may have sinned. And engaging in masturbation, frottage, oral sex, anal sex, bondage, the use of sex toys, partialism, or pornography? Each action will breach a cultural boundary in some church district or settlement, if not in all.

The extent to which these behaviors are censored varies, as does how much they are open to discussion as a violation. Still, it is safe to say that at least some are considered sinful, even if limited to a husband and wife. It is also reasonable to note that these boundaries are frequently violated. In so doing, the guilt that accrues is perhaps minimized, as a shared secret with one's spouse. The power of the collective culture to oversee and critique behavior can be stopped at the bedroom door.

Sex for procreation therefore occurs in tandem with forbidden behaviors for many couples. The ability to rebel with impunity against the heteronormative, however, is limited to one's immediate sexual partner. It becomes more difficult to engage in rebellious behaviors open to observation by the entire community, such as acting out with multiple sexual partners, having extramarital relationships, or engaging in paraphilias that involve nonconsensual interactions (although these do occur, as will be discussed in chapter 8). The efficacy of cultural boundaries can be questioned if members slip their "surly bonds" at the first opportunity.[12] The situation parallels the oft-posed dilemma for parents whose defiant child repeatedly comes home at midnight. The parents then set a limit with an 11 p.m. curfew. The child responds by coming home between 11:15 and 11:30 p.m. Is the curfew working? For some, the answer is no, since the child continues to resist expectations. For others, the answer is yes. The curfew is imperfect, but the child acknowledges the expectation to be home before midnight by returning somewhat earlier than that. The same dilemma arises in prohibiting certain sexual behaviors. If the prohibition limits acting out but does not stop it entirely, is it effective? The answer lies in the perspective of the observer.

The reality is that no social power or control in any culture or society in recorded history has been sufficiently firm to limit all forms of sexual acting out. While queer theory is constructionist and minimizes an emphasis on physiological drive, that drive is still there, and it will manifest itself, demanding satisfaction. The heteronormative can take its place in the foreground. Yet in the background there will always be acting out and subcultures, inappropriate expressions that cannot be completely suppressed.

Breadth and Depth: Amish Awareness of Sexuality

Within Amish culture, knowledge of sexuality can be decidedly and deliberately minimalist. As with any large-scale phenomenon, there is doubtless a bell curve of awareness across the population, but the overt dissemination of sexual data is discouraged. While a breadth of knowledge is inevitable, as natural human curiosity sweeps light into even the most remote and inaccessible corners, prolonged analysis or in-depth investigation is discouraged.

This emphasis on breadth over depth, consistent with a lack of critical thinking, is a hallmark of Amish cognitive processes. Advanced forms of academics, with the knowledge they provide, are dangerous not only because they offer an individual more data than is reasonably needed for a life of service to God, but because they encourage greater intellectual inquiry.[13] This encouragement to avoid critical thought, or deep analysis, extends to the emotional realm. Anxiety and depression are often considered symptoms of a weakened or troubled faith. With further prayer and a stronger commitment to God, say many Amish, these symptoms will fade. The need to explore or analyze the reasons behind such feelings is not as strongly supported. Knowledge via analysis and investigation is reserved for tangible activities. Thus household, mechanical, and industrial puzzles find a ready commitment to problem solving that scientific, emotional, and psychological enigmas do not.

Given the effort to weight knowledge more heavily on the side of pragmatic, as opposed to emotional, problem solving fits with a view in which work supersedes free time as a worthy goal. If pleasure is the reward and the satisfaction obtained from a job well done, then it does not, in and of itself, need to be carefully analyzed. Pleasure is inherent. It can occur while working. A gainfully employed individual experiences satisfaction in doing a job well. Even the delay of pleasure can become a gratification, with the individual taking satisfaction in demonstrating self-control.

The reluctance of the Amish to fully embrace postmodern or even modern technology underscores their physical work ethic and their need to forego excessive comfort. This self-denial is essential to a productive and purposeful life. Experimentation or novelty in sexual behavior falls under the same rubric. It is a slippery slope to hedonism, not an outgrowth of satisfaction in fulfilling God's plan. Sexual energy is controlled by attempting to limit the amount of knowledge available, maintaining strict standards for those who are allowed to engage in sexual behaviors, and hewing to procreation as the primary purpose of sexual activity.

The heteronormative therefore minimizes efforts to deepen or expand sexual pleasure. The Amish limit their involvement in any recreational activities outside of family events as unnecessary excursions into the realm of pleasure. So, too, do they circumscribe an emphasis on the hedonistic aspects of sex. There is no need for an understanding of sex or sexuality beyond the minimal requirements of sexual expression. This expectation reinforces humility, separation from the world, and commitment to the collective culture. The community's inquisitive gaze may stop at the bedroom door, but it can rest comfortably, knowing that the activities it cannot see still do not cross certain boundaries. But how well do these efforts work in a postmodern era of online communication?

How Ya Gonna Keep 'Em Down on the Farm after They've Seen Paree?

The song that titles this section is apt, coming as it did on the heels of soldiers returning from World War I.[14] Amish conscientious objectors from this and subsequent wars were given noncombatant duty but stationed with non-Amish personnel. On their return home, significant numbers failed to join the Amish church after experiencing this taste of the world.[15] In a somewhat similar fashion, the question arises as to whether the culture can retain its heteronormative grip as online communication, including pornography, makes its way into communities via cell phones.[16]

It would be naïve to assume that the Amish have not, since the inception of their communities, known about and engaged in the full range of sexual activities available to human experience. Long before the proliferation of cell phones, and despite the determination by parents not to share sexual information, there was little difference in a mainstream and an Amish child or adolescent's capability to learn the fundamentals of sex, by osmosis if necessary. What still may be different is the proportion of Amish who learn and engage in non-sanctioned behaviors. When they do participate in prohibited sexual acts, they experience guilt and shame. The extent to which they accommodate their guilt seems to vary with the individuals or couples engaging in the activity. Again, the culture discourages open communication about such behavior, so conversations, when they occur, are often hushed disclosures to trusted confidantes.

The ability of this heteronormative expectation to limit sexual activity modeled in the mainstream comes into doubt as cell phones proliferate, and, with them, online pornography. At the same time, the outcome of this proliferation is far from determined. First, by its nature, pornography is derivative. There is little new information to be gleaned from repetitive viewings of sexual activity through these channels. Therefore, while one's breadth of knowledge may expand, further depth is unlikely. Pornography does desensitize the viewer to many facets of sexual behavior,[17] so the guilt and shame traditionally limiting sexual activity within Amish communities may be dissipating rapidly.

Second, although there is an abundance of information about sexual behavior and sexuality available online, Amish culture confines the extent of formal education to the eighth grade. Whether most individuals with this circumscribed academic prowess are genuinely interested in perusing articles for more in-depth information, and the extent to which they comprehend what can be obtained, remain open questions.

Third, the issue of electrical power becomes less important as cell phones and tablets offer more-durable batteries. Nevertheless, while the mainstream culture obtains electricity from the grid, the Amish still rely on less efficient sources. For that reason, the ability to use and charge devices that connect with online data sources requires a greater conservation of power, which may translate to less use. Again, the extent to which this influences the broader dissemination of pornography in the Amish community is unclear.

Still, easier access to adult sexual materials online dilutes the control of the Amish church in the private lives of its members, creating an even larger rift between the collective culture's expectations, which loom in the foreground, and acting out or rebellious behavior in the privacy of one's home. How this will be addressed by the culture's gatekeepers, the clergy, remains to be seen. Their present efforts have largely been ineffective, as cell phone ownership continues to proliferate in many affiliations, despite efforts to minimize their use or ban them altogether.

The paradox of Amish social control over these behaviors is most obvious in the matter of confession. Deviant sexual behaviors are minimally discussed and are a source of tremendous embarrassment. At times, they are acknowledged in confession, relieving the burden of guilt. Relying on confessions known to the author, these include engaging in zoophilia, child sexual abuse, extramarital activity, and masturbation, the latter by both married and unmarried individuals, as well as viewing pornography.

Sexual behavior among the Amish, then, is easily understood at one level. Within the collective culture, the heteronormative purpose of sex is for procreation. No other knowledge is needed, and their cultural mandates anticipate control, ensuring that sex will be used primarily for this purpose. Beneath this paper-thin veneer of expectations, the Amish, as is true in all cultures, demonstrate an intricate and entangled sexuality. The social network that attempts to place controls on behavior can suppress overt dialogue and encourage compliance. It can create discrete discourse and constrain sexual acting out, but it cannot eliminate undesirable behaviors.

Chapter Four

"Knowing" One Another

Ramifications of the Physical Act

While chatting with an Amish father, talk turned to his sons. He mentioned a late adolescent, among the youngest of his children, who had recently joined the church. A compassionate youth, he was frequently sought out by peers for solace and support. "He worried me after church last week," said his father with a frown. I waited, but as no further information was forthcoming, I gave a gentle conversational nudge. With obvious relief, he enlightened me about the boy's behavior.

Another young man, close to his son's age, had made a voluntary confession. Struggling with masturbation, he felt that admitting this to the assembled members would provide the support needed to overcome this impure habit. After the service, his son approached this peer and offered empathy in the face of a common struggle. "I'm afraid the bishop will hear about it and want [my son] to confess too," his father said. "Sometimes he doesn't think about what he's doing before he acts!"

Sympathy, or at least commiseration, is common when we consider the sexual troubles of others. The legendary comedian Rodney Dangerfield kept the following joke as a staple in his repertoire: "I get no respect. No respect. I went to buy a used car, I found my wife's dress in the backseat!" The difficulty in maintaining sexual boundaries and the discomfort attending that effort strike a common chord. For the Amish it is not just the boundary against illicit sexual contact that is zealously guarded. As a collective culture, determined to distance itself from the enticements of the world, the risks posed by "knowing" each other are much broader, encompassing acts that most of mainstream culture dismisses as harmless.[1] This chapter deconstructs these prohibitions and sanctions. For those who fail to rein in the risk their sins create, there are consequences designed to return them to a proper relationship with God.

Discipline and Amish Life

The Ordnung has been mentioned repeatedly, but in a chapter addressing discipline, it deserves a closer look. The book *The Amish* has one of the best descriptions of this touchstone of daily life:[2]

A communal spirituality that focuses on the daily practices of faith requires common lifestyle understandings for the Gmay [church]. What is striking about Amish religion is how it crisscrosses dimensions of daily life, from dress codes to the use of technology, from education to political participation. "We must submit to each other in the application of biblical principles that are not specifically spelled out in the scriptures," says one Amish leader.

The common guidelines for Amish life, known as the Ordnung, provide a blueprint for expected and forbidden behavior. Although the Ordnung is typically an oral tradition, ministers in some groups keep a written record of it. This body of interpretation—both oral and written—gives guidance on moral issues that are not addressed directly by Scripture as well as practical applications of biblical principles. The Ordnung typically includes guidelines for dress, buggies, technology, home décor, sports, and similar matters. Although leaders recommend guidelines, they are only binding when ratified by the congregation.

In one sense, the Ordnung communicates the collective advice of the Gmay. But it is more than advice. The Ordnung requires obedience because the Amish believe that it flows from the moral discernment of the church, which is blessed by the spirit of Christ and endorsed by heaven. Yet because of its oral and unsystematic character, the Ordnung is pliable and adaptable. A good Ordnung, the Amish say, is readily accepted

by members and promotes harmony and unity in the redemptive community. Members who intentionally stray from guidelines will receive
repeated admonitions before they face excommunication. . . . The Ordnung's central role in providing moral guidance reveals the priority of
faithful practice over doctrinal belief in the Amish religion.

The importance of the Ordnung in the life of the community ensures that the heteronormative is woven into the social fabric. Sexual
mores do not stand alone, or even in context with other values. They
are interconnected with those values, so there is a seamless blend not
only between the sexual and the social, but also between sexuality
and spirituality. Thus for some, an act as personal as self-stimulation
can be brought to the attention of the church as a spiritual demon to
be conquered through the awareness and support of the group.

The Earliest Struggle

Masturbation as a sexual outlet assumes an outsized moral significance across history.[3] For the Amish, it remains fixed in an early
twentieth-century view, an autoerotic fascination at its most dangerous
in adolescence. An example of this attitude appeared in an Amish
periodical, *Young Companion*. A product of the Amish publishing
house Pathway, the magazine targets their youth. In addition, Pathway's flagship magazine, *Family Life*, is one of the most influential
periodicals written by and for Plain people.[4] In one issue of *Young
Companion*, the editors included two essays that admonish adolescents on the dangers inherent in masturbation. The first excerpt is
taken from an article titled "A Way to Escape":[5]

> Are you a boy who is struggling? Struggling to win over sin? Impu-
> rity? Immorality? Self-abuse? Are you struggling with these? Keep on
> reading.
>   I, too, was there. I was living in sin. I wanted to do what was right, but
> it was so hard. I struggled and struggled. I thought I had won, and then
> I failed again. . . .
>   But think. Where will you be in eternity? Do you want victory? Con-

fess to your parents or to a minister. Please don't keep trying and failing on your own. Don't keep it a secret. Get help.

The second excerpt, from the same edition, is taken from an article titled "The Battle Leading Up:"[6]

This is the story of a young man's struggle with impurity. . . . We see a young man standing at a fork in the road. One branch leads down and the other climbs up. This young man takes the path down. When he started downward, he gained speed rapidly. . . .

The bad news is that I ever began. Had I never given in to that first bad influence, it might have turned out much differently. But do not despair if you cannot make it in the first year. It took me over three years to achieve this goal. I had to learn the hard way that if we give Satan our little finger, he will not stop at that.

These essays are unusual, because the magazine rarely addresses sexuality. Still, when the topic is confronted—as is true with most efforts to provide a moral compass—there is no emphasis placed on underlying dynamics, the troubling contradictions in making correct life decisions, or the trauma that historical events can inflict, thus complicating the struggle. Instead, there is a clear-cut decision. The author offers breadth, that is, the choice in the immediate moment and its moral consequences, but not depth, in either an analysis or in historical implications. An adolescent must choose to either engage in self-induced pleasure, a violation of the will of God, or renounce sin and live in purity.

True to their beliefs, the writer(s) of these stories also assume that the boy (certainly not an Amish girl!) struggling with this temptation is unable to make consistent, good choices on his own. He requires the community and its collective support, in conjunction with a prayerful attitude, to overcome the pitfall. This is the value of public confession. It brings an individual's struggle to the larger group, and the larger group into that personal struggle.

Nonetheless, because masturbation is such a common behavior

among adolescents,[7] it gives rise to widely different responses among churches and settlements. Some youths struggling with this behavior perceive it as a sin and choose to confess their moral weakness. Others engage in a discussion with friends or confidantes on its morality but avoid public confession. (One young man wept with relief when he shared his struggle with an older friend, who normalized the behavior.) In some settlements, group masturbation becomes a rite of passage, while in others even the private act of autoeroticism is a horrible sin.

The Amish concern over autoerotic behavior is notable, because it predates church membership. A late adolescent or young adult who is single and joins the church agrees to the Ordnung and accepts the need for confession. But here, an emphasis is also placed on younger adolescents, whose control remains the responsibility of the family and does not yet require formal discipline by the church. Heteronormative expectations are instilled at an early age.

In addition, absence is again notable. The Amish are aware that adolescent females masturbate. In a patriarchal society the importance of female sexuality is diminished. Power and control in the sexual realm are assumed to remain with the male.[8] Therefore, it is the male's sexual behavior that is of primary concern, as defined by heteronormative expectations.

The Broad View of Discipline

Few persons raised outside this close-knit band of Christian sojourners join the Amish church.[9] Of those who do, no published study systematically polls their most difficult adjustment. Anecdotally, the top of the list is not populated by the need to forsake the convenience of owning a motor vehicle. Nor is it the daily struggle with the painstaking contraptions necessary to accommodate life without electricity. Not even the demand of learning a new dialect in order to easily converse with one's confidantes ranks foremost. At the top is the comparative lack of privacy, as independence and autonomy, so prized and characteristic of citizenship in the United States or Canada, is replaced by a collective that owes its allegiance to God Almighty and exists in service to him. The Amish governing system assumes that members of the community work together for the common good. Thus, while they retain independence in financial and family relationships, the code of conduct under which they live even their most private moments is regulated and monitored by the community itself.

Lest this begin to bear the sinister traits of a cult,[10] the Amish employ measures to ensure that no one enters this collective covenant without full awareness and agreement. Rumspringa, the adolescent period of exploration normally beginning at age sixteen, allows these young adults (as they are then considered) to step away from family and church, look back, and contemplate their choice. At this stage, if they elect to turn away, there is grief but resignation on the part of their family and community, especially if they join a church with similar theological beliefs, such as a branch of the Mennonites. A young adult deciding to join the church must first take classes with the clergy (usually the bishop) for several Sundays prior to the sacrament of baptism. These steps toward membership frame the solemnity and importance of the pending vows, as the individual is expected to remain a member for a lifetime.

Voluntary and forewarned though this membership choice may be, there are still strong currents that sweep a young person in an Amish home into the waiting arms of the church. Likewise, there are powerful forces that mitigate against leaving once someone becomes a member of the fold. For a person raised Amish, in a family of approximately seven children,[11] surrounded by an even larger extended family and sheltered from extensive contact with the world, a decision to leave is far less common than a decision to stay. Approximately 85 percent of Amish children will join the church, so the majority make a commitment to this spiritual and cultural group.[12] Even those who leave retain a strong sense of Amish identity.[13]

Such a decision is not surprising. From birth, children are steeped in Amish culture. A Pennsylvania German dialect is their first language,[14] so communication with persons outside the settlement is limited until

entering school and attaining fluency in English. The message that
the world poses a threat is an overt and covert theme throughout
their lives. "The world," meaning all that is not Amish, dresses, acts,
and speaks differently, and it adheres to a fundamentally dissimilar,
and presumed lesser, set of values. When those of the world interact
with the Amish, these dealings are monitored, limited, and met with
a measure of caution and reserve. Such boundaries become ingrained,
essential even to the identity of those adolescents wavering in the
decision of whether to remain Amish for a lifetime.

Yet what happens once one is committed, joining with the understanding that God is Creator and Jesus his son is the hope for salvation? How does the church hold sway over its membership? As noted
earlier, Amish doctrinal concerns are focused on the practical much
more than on the theological. They emphasize order and authority
and reflect themes of discipleship. The administration of the church is
formulated on these principles. Theirs is a paternal hierarchy that emphasizes obedience. Those who violate the Ordnung are observed and
reported, and discipline is meted by the clergy as deemed appropriate.
This would conjure the image of a police state, were it not balanced
by unwavering support in the face of trauma, or even less desperate
needs. The primary intent of the Ordnung is not to oppress one's
family, friends, and neighbors under the watchful eye of Big Brother.
Its purpose is to keep the community on the straight and narrow. To
do so requires loving forbearance, discipline, and nurturing support.

At the same time, the church must accommodate change in its rules
and expectations. The physical environment, civil laws, and social customs in the mainstream are in flux. These external pressures impinge
on the Amish and force their culture to adapt to shifting demands.
Change can also occur from within. Members chafe at rules that
seem outdated. Or perhaps, instead of a rule that no longer fits, there
may be a groundswell of disapproval toward a particular standard.
A minor revolt emerges as members test the determination of their
leadership to stand firm. These changes are often isolated attempts
to make a statement, involving one family or only a few members.

Or they may be gradual, tentative movements away from the norm. For example, bicycles are permitted by many church districts in the Elkhart-LaGrange area of Indiana. It is not uncommon to see an Amish rider on a new and different model of bike. Perhaps one, and then several more, will make the shift to this new design. Over the course of several seasons these outliers will either proliferate, indicating that the Ordnungs of many churches have approved of this modification in transportation, or they will disappear, signaling that they were too worldly to be accepted.

Minor infractions are overlooked or addressed informally. Despite appearances, the church does not micromanage the actions of its members. As behaviors escalate into more serious violations, several choices become available. Members of the Amish church are free to express themselves in areas not covered by the Ordnung, but there is an overarching expectation for cooperation that supersedes specific rules. Perhaps a lawn is not mowed frequently enough. Or farm machinery is used for a purpose beyond normal boundaries. On off Sundays, when members are expected to visit the churches of those in other Gmays, a family might stay home. If enough of these minor violations occur, the fractious members are alerted that they are drifting out of compliance with the collective spirit. In many settlements this remains an informal awareness. Other churches practice the more formal *Unfriddah*.[15] Those experiencing the shame of Unfriddah remain welcome to participate fully in the community and the church. Still, there is a distance, a formality to social interactions, and a hesitation in sharing fully. This social chill sends a warning, serving as a low-level reminder that the community goal is unity. The manner of conveying this distance varies across churches and settlements, as does the use of Unfriddah itself.

There is no clear dividing line between attitudes and behaviors that receive an informal rebuke and those that rise to the level of Unfriddah. Likewise, there is no precise distinction between those that invoke Unfriddah and those that require confession. Confession varies by affiliation, settlement, and church.[16] Some are voluntary confessions, as in the vignette that begins this chapter. In these cases, the penitent recognizes a sin against either biblical expectations or the Ordnung and chooses to acknowledge it to the church. In other instances, the transgression is observed or reported to the clergy. The sinner is then confronted and asked to confess. The style of confession conforms to the nature of the sin and the attitude of the sinner. For a minor transgression and a repentant member, confession may be informal and private, shared only with the minister. For more serious sins or with resistant members, confession can occur in church. The penitent may be asked to sit, stand, or, for the most serious infractions, kneel. The congregation usually affirms the proposed action in response to the confession, either in prior discussion between the ministers or as a part of the confession itself.

Although the need to confess can be anxiety provoking, confession itself often serves as a purge for remorse and guilt. The Amish believe that sin, once confessed, is forgiven. The ritual therefore becomes a powerful tool for emotional healing. If the penitent does not receive immediate forgiveness, the bishop can, with the affirmation of the Gmay, either impose a *Bann* or excommunicate the offending member. Many churches differentiate between a short Bann, lasting approximately two to six weeks, and a long Bann, considered to be more resolute. A short Bann applies to sins that are too severe for immediate forgiveness; individuals who are resistant or stubborn in accepting the discipline of the church; or, at times, those who seek a severe punishment for their own failure. A long Bann is more frequently used when members defy the Ordnung and force the church to make a choice regarding their membership. Even though most individuals accept this as a permanent ban, penitents can request consideration for reinstatement at any time if they are willing to confess their sins, change the behavior(s) in question, and return to an appropriate way of life.

Amish seekers are aware that, in requesting membership, they subjugate sexual behavior to the expectations of the Ordnung, the vehicle to maintain the heteronormative. Unacceptable sexual outlets, if discovered, will be labeled as sinful, be subject to censure, and possibly induce a demand for confession. If the shame and guilt surrounding these hidden behaviors create an overwhelming need to voluntarily confess, there will still be censure, although less so than if the behavior is discovered and reported. This is social control that all Amish will have observed, modeled from childhood forward. Only church members will have seen an actual confession. Still, in the easily accessed communication of a high-context culture, children and adolescents will have an understanding of what confession involves.

The heteronormative of this collective culture is powerful enough that sexual acting out and sexual minorities do not create internal subcultures that exert pressure against these norms. Aside from its primary marital use for procreation, sexual *behavior* itself remains deviant, sinful, and subject to condemnation. The Ordnung remains unequivocal in its refusal to sanction even gradual changes in these expectations.

The Temptation to Stray: Sex Outside of Marriage

In mainstream culture, 15–20 percent of married persons engage in extra-relationship sexual activities, as the attitudes decrying such behavior continue to decline.[17] There is no statistical data to support the frequency of extramarital relationships among the Amish. From anecdotal information, such acting out occurs less often than in the general population. While it would be uplifting to believe that the reason for this is grounded in stronger moral standards, a collective culture allows less freedom for persons to participate in illicit interactions without discovery. Therefore, Amish society creates a predilection to engage in relationships that are more easily hidden than these. An Amish/English tryst is much more discrete than an Amish/Amish one. Cross-cultural romantic liaisons are more difficult to monitor and control and, hence, are presumably more common. Extramarital liaisons, both Amish/English and Amish/Amish, are often the impetus for the tentative couple (or the Amish half of a couple) to legitimize the relationship by accepting the Bann in order to start a life together. After all, the church brooks no halfway measures.

Marriage is a lifetime commitment, and a partner does not have the option of divorce to marry a new love. The choice is stark. Renounce the romantic interest outside the marriage, confess and ask forgiveness, and embrace the current wife, family, and church once again. Or renounce the collective culture in its entirety.

Any sexual relationship outside of marriage carries the same weight of sin, but from a pragmatic standpoint clergy are more tolerant of some behaviors. Youth in Rumspringa are nominally freed from the strictures of parents and do not face the onus of confession, since they are not yet church members. Therefore, if they engage in sexual behavior, the church often chooses to ignore their sin. Prayers turn heavenward for their safety and salvation, but their autonomy during this period means that they are guided by their conscience and by whatever guilt the community can instill with its overarching presence. There is no proscriptive discipline to be meted out, at least until they join the church. At that point, some clergy ask for confession. Others avoid addressing this period in the young people's lives, preferring to see them start life anew.

Sexual activity, alcohol, and drug use are far from being universally tolerated,[18] but "gangs" of Amish youth vary in their degree of acting out once in Rumspringa.[19] For example, in the Lancaster, Pennsylvania, settlement, approximately one-half of the youth gangs are supervised by parents, who ensure a more modest experience.[20] The remaining groups include youth who act out in significant ways. While gangs in other settlements are rarely supervised, they demonstrate a similar distribution from "mild" to "wild." Greater sexual activity occurs in the wilder gangs, accompanying a more prevalent use of alcohol and other drugs. Amish males who engage in such activity are less likely to be censored than Amish females, and some females participating in these wilder groups report frustration when they are assumed to be willing sexual partners for their male peers.

The heteronormative during Rumspringa is therefore much more pleasure based than at any other developmental stage. Constraints are lifted, and adolescents (extending, in some settlements, to young adults) have the opportunity to venture onto the devil's playground of the world. For a plurality of these youth, hedonism is their temporary purpose, and both substance use and casual sexual encounters are the norm. Unfortunately, the patriarchal influence continues to hold sway. Perhaps even more so than under the watchful eye of the Ordnung, females risk subjugation instead of voluntary submission to males, since male dominance is unfettered.[21] Nonetheless, the overwhelming majority of these acting-out adolescents join the church and acquiesce once again to the strictures of a conservative morality over their sexuality.

During this period, many couples intensify the seriousness of their dating. Privacy in an Amish home remains at a premium. Parents, grandparents, siblings, and extended family members constantly move throughout the house, and there is little place for a dating couple to find privacy, other than in a bedroom.[22] If a suitor visits from a geographic distance, even if only of several miles, it can be more practical for him to return home in the morning, rather than start home late at night. Therefore, there are occasions when a young Amish couple spends time together in bed, albeit fully clothed. Their privacy there is not complete, and the purpose of such behavior is not to allow a sexual tryst. Instead, there is recognition that a developing relationship needs a time and a place to flourish without being under watchful eye of the family, and a bedroom is the logical choice.

That purpose stated, human nature is . . . human nature. Dating couples usually stop short of intercourse, but they do engage in sexual play. Amish moral strictures can create guilt about their behavior and limit the frequency, duration, and specific acts in which they engage, as is true in the larger culture.[23] It also seems that once marriage has been decided upon, sexual behavior increases, but this is a highly individualized choice. Injunctions against sexual behavior limit some but not all such actions.

The decision to join the church does not put a stop to all acting out. Sexual trysts may continue at Rumspringa parties, and the clergy may remain more tolerant, provided the members are single. Until

a youth signals an intention to marry and start a family, the need to
demonstrate more mature attitudes and behaviors is not as pressing
from the standpoint of either family or clergy. The exception is if
the female in an Amish dating couple becomes pregnant. There is a
modicum of shame in having thus been caught engaging in sexual
behavior outside of marriage. In such situations a truncated wedding
occurs, instead of a full day of celebration. In some settlements this
wedding occurs on a Sunday, not during the week, as is customary.
Once the transgressing pair are married and established, their sin is
forgiven and the new family is welcomed into the church and the
community.

Fertility Practices

The Amish adhere to nature's plan, including intercourse and a
subsequent pregnancy, should it occur. Still, contraception is an area in
which the heteronormative expectations in the foreground can be defied
in the background. The Amish discourage artificial means of limiting
conception. Devices and techniques violate the majority of Ordnungs,
including hormonal means (pills, implants, injections, patches, vaginal
rings, and hormonal intrauterine devices, or IUDs), barriers (male and
female condoms, cervical caps, diaphragms, non-hormonal IUDs, and
contraceptive sponges), coitus interruptus, sterilization (vasectomy or
tubal ligation), and emergency contraception (commonly known as
the morning-after pill). Tolerated methods include fertility awareness
(rhythm methods) and lactational amenorrhea (reduction in female
fertility postpartum and during breastfeeding), since these capitalize
on natural bodily responses.

In the background, contraception is more frequently used. A study
of women of childbearing age in the Lancaster settlement found that
20 percent endorsed some form of protection.[24] Anecdotal data from
Pennsylvania and Indiana settlements identify a greater use of contraception to manage and space births, rather than as an effort to reduce
the number of children per se. Non-hormonal IUDs and condoms are
more commonly requested, and sterilization is rarely a consideration.

Therefore, the heteronormative expectation dampens but does not extinguish the options.

Such gradual acceptance is consistent with the Amish style of slowly embracing technological advances or making any change to the Ordnung. The variety of contraceptive techniques and devices now available, combined with their surreptitious use by some Amish, makes this a cautious approach, where its impact is difficult to observe. Further, the heteronormative assumes that sex is primarily for procreation. Contraception subverts this imperative and, by its nature, disrupts the natural order. The role of Amish culture as a bastion of Christian principles would be significantly weakened by a mass introduction of contraceptive devices. The strength of the heteronormative in this area is imperative, but, much like the battle against cell phones, contraceptive use is an insidious attack, borne out in an area that is difficult to confront directly.

The long-term effect of this introduction of contraception is difficult to predict for the Amish. Data indicate that more-conservative settlements have a higher birthrate,[25] so that, consistent with logic, more-progressive groups appear to be embracing this technology first. The mean number of children in a family now stands at seven. There is anecdotal evidence that young Amish couples are delaying the start of their families and reducing the frequency with which they add children. To do so in numbers significant enough to impact average family size or the spacing of children would indicate a widespread use of artificial contraception.

The issue thus raised again becomes the degree to which the culture can enforce its values, not a polarized choice of all or none. Americans experience a birthrate hovering at 1.72 children in a lifetime, and this number continues to decline.[26] Therefore, Amish couples procreate about four times as rapidly as the mainstream. If cultural pressure cannot dictate that couples avoid artificial contraception entirely, it can pressure them to limit the options, as well as the duration and frequency of their use, compared with those in the mainstream.

Increased contraceptive use and efficacy could also lead to the empowerment of women.[27] A dramatic decrease in the number of children per family could open roles for them that have been inaccessible, due to the demands of childcare and family life. As has been demonstrated repeatedly, the introduction of contraception in a society leads to a notable uptick in the power and prestige held by females. Their expanded roles as businesswomen and even entrepreneurs, their increased mobility and presence in the community, and flexibility in their traditional gender roles would require a significant change in their cultural presence. This would create a substantial threat for the patriarchy.

Such a change would not alter the Amish view of childbirth, however. A pregnancy is considered a gift from God. Even if a fetus is identified as exhibiting pronounced disabilities or impairments, an abortion is unthinkable. During pregnancy, the Amish do not perceive a fetus. They perceive a child, a responsibility provided by God, theirs to offer care and love to from the moment of conception forward. Therefore, there can be no thought of terminating the pregnancy. There *are* extremely rare exceptions to this belief. If the choice becomes the life of the mother or the life of the child, the parents may decide to abort, albeit not necessarily with the church's knowledge. If the pregnancy is the result of a particularly horrific sexual act, such as incest or sexual assault, an abortion may be obtained quietly, again without the awareness of the church. The Amish may also turn to "powwowing," an occult or sympathy healing that lingers on the fringes of the culture and is largely held in disfavor.[28] In this practice, a family member or close confidante may attempt to induce an abortion by relatively passive means, using herbs, incantations, or a combination of both.

The decision to abort, whether legally, through powwowing, or some other avenue, is an extremely rare event and is deeply troubling for all involved. By taking what the Amish consider to be a viable human life, they violate a central tenet of their beliefs, and the trauma involved, both for the pregnant female and any complicit family, is longstanding and devastating.

There are also Amish couples who desperately desire to have a child and are unable to do so. Plagued by fertility issues, they experience pervasive pressures from family, friends, church, and community as time passes and they have not brought a child into the world. While single individuals and childless couples have a place in the community and can be respected and loved, the cycle of life is anticipated to include children.

Still, the same expectations apply for infertility as they do when a couple is anxious to avoid procreation. Nature is respected, and artificial inducements to fertility are disdained. Nonetheless, there is greater tolerance for medical assistance to assess and assist with fertility than for contraception. Few Amish utilize more than basic assisted reproductive technology (ART).[29] A limited number try artificial insemination, particularly since it can be practiced in the home. Rarely does a couple having trouble conceiving practice in vitro fertilization, and no Amish couple to date (known to this author) has allowed a surrogate pregnancy.

The heteronormative emphasis in Amish culture remains on a natural and God-inspired process of procreation, interrupted as little as possible by human artifice. Even when contraception is used, the methods are the least invasive, most natural, and are as close to compliance with the Ordnung as possible. This emphasis is a logical outgrowth of the expectation that sexual activity occurs for the purpose of reproduction. Social power and control fit seamlessly with the belief that God's plan for creation should be carried through, from intercourse to insemination to the pregnancy itself. It also maintains the submissive role of women. This underlines the ultimate power of the culture, as it flows directly from the word of God and drives behavior to conform to the expectations of scripture.

Pregnancy and Delivery

It may seem improbable in twenty-first-century North America, but there are Amish women who proceed through pregnancy, delivery, and postnatal care without visiting a physician or a hospital.[30]

Relatively few go to this extreme, even among the multiple births for women in Plain communities, but there are nevertheless a dedicated number who choose this route. They do so by relying on midwives, many of them licensed or certified, who handle births in the home or in birthing centers.[31] In doing so, pregnant women remain sheltered within their communities and avoid the alien expectations of a hospital delivery room and its staff. The use of midwives in the community also demonstrates faith in the safety God provides, which the use of a hospital does not.

I drove an Amish woman from her home to the midwife's, in order to visit the place where she had delivered most of her children. She described taking the buggy with her husband on what was, by horse, about a one-hour drive. Once at the midwife's home, we were met by a kindly older woman who showed us the rooms in which the expectant mothers were housed. The Amish mother described the care she received and the wonderful meal she was served after the ordeal of giving birth was over. The opportunity to have her children in this quaint house, far from medical assistance, but deep within the settlement in which she lived, was important for her sense of security. The heteronormative included a strong injunction against trusting the world, even in matters of the health of herself and her unborn child.

Birthing centers are a compromise between home care and a large, impersonal hospital. Normally located within the settlement, they offer trained staff who assist with prenatal care and delivery, as well as monitor and assess the pregnancy and birth with a greater level of nursing sophistication than a home-based midwife. Because of their proximity within the settlement and their small size in comparison with a hospital, the atmosphere in a birthing center is more convivial, relaxed, and secure for an Amish mother-to-be.

Some women still prefer a hospital setting. This is particularly true for a first pregnancy, or if there is a history of prior complications. As women age and births become more difficult, or as postpartum recovery is longer, they may return to the hospital. (This may also reflect the greater financial stability of an older couple.) Hospitals near Amish settlements are aware of the needs of their Amish patients and often accommodate these concerns.

New mothers receive special attention from the extended family. They are supported by parents, siblings, and aunts as they negotiate their first steps into parenthood. The level of assistance wanes with the second, third, and fourth child, but the extended family remains aware that extra help is needed. This support gives an essential message to the young couple. It serves as a prolonged blessing, another rite of passage, as family lifts them on their journey into parenthood. The young couple may face having a new life in their midst, but they are not alone.

"Knowing" One Another and the Formation of Identity

There is an insidious pressure, starting from birth through entry into Rumspringa and during all of that liminal period, to join the Amish church. Nothing is covert. Amish parents long for their children to choose to become Amish and make no secret of their hopes. A principal ingredient in the pressure brought to bear on youth is the indoctrination of sexual mores and values. These embody an insistence to conform not only to a fundamental Christian perspective, but also to an Amish perspective. This includes the intricate steps to the dance that plays out between tolerated and accepted behaviors that shape the heteronormative background and foreground. The guilt that arises in violating these rules can be divested only through the support and understanding of fellow Amish. Certain thoughts and behaviors are absolutely forbidden. Therefore they either must be banished from conscious awareness, or they must become an identity that is carefully compartmentalized, isolated from one's identification with the collective culture. These are aspects of the self, of the recognition of who one is as a person, that make sense only to another who has lived the life.

That understanding is made even more important by the superficiality of their sexual knowledge (see chapter 3). The Amish do not analyze or investigate sexual behavior in depth. Instead, they avoid understanding the dynamics underlying sexual acts and content themselves with addressing the action in the immediate moment.

Consider the fear and anxiety that are natural accompaniments to so many relationships in mainstream culture. A couple meet and discover a romantic attraction. As the relationship becomes more intense, they spend more time together, including more overnight visits. At some point they discuss the option of cohabitating, rather than maintaining two dwellings. As the relationship progresses, or as an outcome of agreeing to move it to the next level, they consider marriage. Children are unlikely to be a long-term interference with the mother's career, if she chooses to pursue one. They hope, as do all couples, for permanence, but they are realists. If a marriage proves unworkable, divorce occurs about half the time. For some, another concern is the possibility that one of them will find employment in another geographic location, precipitating a decision about whether to move and risk a loss of income and career for the other partner. These What ifs? are a direct outgrowth of individualism and choice, the cornerstones of mainstream culture.

An Amish couple also experience anxiety and fear. In this case, such emotions result from considering a lifetime together. There will be no cohabitation prior to marriage. Even if they are from different settlements, the couple can find enough people who know their spouse-to-be for each to become well versed in the other's history and background. Children are the mother's career, along with care of the home. Moving in conjunction with marriage may involve a new dwelling in the existing settlement but no loss of nearby friends or family. If relocation to a new settlement does occur, kin connections might be to either the husband's or the wife's family. The potential for an extramarital relationship is virtually nonexistent in comparison with a non-Amish couple.

Identity for these two sets of couples as they begin a life together also diverges markedly. The path down which a committed relationship will take them involves struggles with emotional intimacy, but there is a vast cultural divide that dictates the options for resolving these struggles. For the mainstream couple, their task is to find their roles as individuals within this newly merged life. What does it mean for one's unique identity to be a marital partner? For the Amish couple, issues of identity occur, but many facets of their roles are already culturally prescribed. Aspects of their sense of self, much like their clothes, have been preselected. The struggles over what it means to develop a vulnerability, a trust, and a deepening love for another human being remain the same. Yet the ways in which these struggles play out will be dissimilar within the two cultures. The heteronormative ideal within Amish society is much more pervasive—indeed, invasive—than within the mainstream.

Perhaps if the understanding of sexual behavior could itself be parsed, sheared off, and isolated, it would be easier to loose the powerful bonds of the culture that created it. But it, too, is interwoven with the larger purpose of living as an Amish person. God has ordained that lifestyle, and sex and sexuality are encompassed in its larger meaning. Provided that sexual behavior ultimately results in pregnancy and birth, other forms of sexual expression, if culturally disapproved, are either practiced discretely, with the accompanying shame mitigated by sharing the secret with one's partner, or become taboo. The identity that Amish culture allows the individual to adopt is stamped with a collective seal of approval. Beyond that approval? No other identity is allowed to exist, at least within the social order.

As shown in the following chapters, this formation of identity becomes an essential component in the creation of gender roles, expressions of intimacy, manifestations of paraphilias, and sexual conduct outside the purview of Amish standards. It is also crucial in concerns that arise as the Amish observe the rapidly changing landscape of sexuality in North American mainstream culture today.

Chapter Five

Gender Roles

Housework and Harvesting

Submissive women. Gender roles that leave no room for questions. These are often considered hallmarks of Amish life. And in some ways, they are. Yet, as years of involvement with their culture have taught me, while the roles may be inflexible, performing them is not.

I visited an Amish farm, to be told by one of the children that her mother was in the barn. An adolescent son was renowned for his skills with hard-to-break horses, and it was not unusual to find an uncontrollable animal housed there. As little as I understood the process, it had still been amazing to spend time watching him approach and calm a skittish horse. Across the barnyard came the sounds of snorts, neighs, restless hooves, and the thud of flesh against wooden walls. Assuming he was at work, I pulled open the barn door, only to find the woman of the house running a colt on a short lead, her face aglow, skirt flying, pacing herself nimbly alongside. The animal finally tired and stood, panting. She passed a hand down its neck and spoke softly in dialect. The animal calmed, and she walked it back to its stall. Seeing me for the first time she stopped, breathless as well. "I just love doing that," she said, and with appropriate modesty explained that her son had gained his horse-breaking skills from her.

This is perhaps the most blatant instance of gender role reversal I have observed. In another turnabout example, I met with a father/husband who was to serve as a guide for the day in a distant settlement. Before leaving his home we visited the laundry room, stacked floor to ceiling with family clothing. He removed one load from the washer and put another in its place. "I'm helping my wife," he said, explaining that she was caring for her elderly father and would return later that morning. He had been sorting laundry and washing it since "standing up" (the Amish term for the morning routine).

The story above triggered a reminisce from a fellow academic who works with the Amish. He recalled a minister raised in a family composed solely of sons. Because of this, as a boy he was assigned the chore of cooking. He not only became adept in the kitchen, but also enjoyed the role of cook. Once married, he discovered that his wife disliked that chore, so across their years together he assumed the task of preparing meals. Despite his willingness to shoulder this one area of female responsibilities, other gender-assigned tasks remained as they should.

What becomes noteworthy about these vignettes is not the discovery that an Amish woman breaks horses or an Amish man cooks (and both love these tasks), or that an Amish man would deign to do laundry. Amish men and women frequently crisscross boundaries and take on chores assigned to the other gender, assuming a duty not in their purview. But, lest the heteronormative ideal be subverted, they understand that the tasks they are performing are not their primary responsibility.

The patriarchy embedded in Amish culture relies on these carefully defined gender roles. The increasingly blurred heteronormative of male and female responsibilities in mainstream culture is a fundamental threat to this patriarchal system. Feminist victories mean a more egalitarian position for women, easing years of social and financial inequity and submission. Spectators can now watch high school football games with female players, and drivers can pass a female running a bulldozer without feeling, like Alice, that they have stepped through the looking glass. (Granted, no man has graced the swimsuit issue of *Sports Illustrated*, but give it time. Give it time . . .) Still, Amish culture has largely taken the advances of females in stride.

For example, few express concerns when treated by a female health-care professional.

A greater threat to the patriarchy comes not from the advance of a feminist agenda, but from the advances of sexual minorities. "So God created man in his own image, in the image of God created he him; male and female created he them" (Genesis 1:27, KJV). This verse, and the many others perceived as supporting it, are read as literal descriptions of creation and a blueprint for relationships. With the legalization of gay marriage and the tolerance, if not acceptance, among so many subcultures for gays, gender nonconformity, and transgender status, queer theory predicts that the Amish heteronormative will respond exactly as it does, with an immediate and unequivocal backlash. As a current minority, the Amish argue for the inviolability of the patriarchy and its accompanying binary gender roles. If these binary roles are diffused, patriarchal authority is weakened.

What are these roles? A woman is ordained by God to be submissive to a man. Conversely, a man is ordained to be a leader in the church, the family, and business. It is tempting to stop here and deconstruct gender hierarchy as tightly sorted layers. In reality, however, gender submission is multifaceted, with masculine and feminine social control overlaying, intertwined with, and at times parallel to layers of authority. This chapter examines these ramifications and heteronormative expectations of gender roles and gender equality. Of concern is the risk for this intertwined authority to become less multifaceted and more tightly layered in response to heteronormative pressures from a mainstream culture that is increasingly permissive.

Early Hierarchy: The Preschool Years

The interpersonal system of an Amish household functions far differently than its mainstream American and Canadian counterparts. Donald Kraybill has estimated that an Amish individual counts 250 persons as family members.[1] A significant number of these will assist in caring for newborns and infant children. In doing so, the model teaches that many older extended family members, not just the nuclear family, invest in those who are younger and take on a playmate, caretaker, or combined role. An older, same-gender sibling assumes responsibility for the next in line, monitoring and teaching appropriate behavior, dress, and grooming.[2]

Care for infants and the youngest children is initially provided during worship by both parents, even though women sit on one side of the room during the service, and men on the other. Gender separation is relaxed as a mother holds a baby boy or a father a baby girl. As children mature, they sit with their appropriate gender. In the same manner, a child is assigned chores based on gender-appropriate and gender-neutral responsibilities, although that work is not confined to gender-appropriate chores. Modeled behavior includes assisting where needed within a large and bustling family system. But there is an understanding that a brother is merely helping a sister, a daughter a father, or the like, and not assuming responsibilities rightfully belonging to the other by virtue of gender, as noted in the vignettes at the start of this chapter.

Appropriate gender roles are modeled and taught during the formative years in the context of this broad, top-down model. Children learn to respect those who are older, not because of their age per se, but because they have knowledge to impart, doing so in a practical manner on a daily basis. Elders also provide safety and security, another essential theme in the Amish hierarchy. They contain, as well as separate children from, the risks and dangers inherent in interacting with the world.

This early socialization affirms the role of the individual. Assimilation into the collective, and the means of gaining knowledge and awareness necessary in a high-context group, are internalized by these early experiences. Also embedded here is a beginning definition of one's gender role. There is room for individual interpretation, but the broad parameters of an Amish male and female are defined, every bit as much as the parameters of the clothing these children will wear. In this way, the intricacies of the patriarchy come into clearer focus.

The Teaching Hierarchy: Scholars and Beyond

As Amish children enter academics, particularly those who become "scholars" (i.e., students in Amish schools), they find it modeled on a microcosm of the hierarchy. In the words of Karen Johnson-Weiner, "Old Order schools do not attempt to prepare children to be knowledgeable citizens of the broader society, for the Old Orders assume an identity that rejects many of the responsibilities—and questions many of the rights and privileges—that mainstream Americans associate with citizenship."[3] In school, Amish children are now under the tutelage of adults who have not only practical knowledge to impart, but also formal education. As scholars, they are expected to assimilate and retain this information and comport themselves in a manner appropriate to their culture. This includes ongoing lessons, both implicit and explicit, about gender roles.

There is nothing startling about these expectations. After all, preschoolers and kindergartners, at an age younger than these scholars, begin school in the mainstream culture with the same expectations. Public school students, however, are welcomed by teachers with high school diplomas and a minimum of four years of college that includes training, not only in how to teach, but also in child development and young people's needs. There will be no distinction between the authority or status of teaching staff based on gender, and women have equality with men. Children are placed in classes with (at best) a few friends, as well as a largely unknown group of peers. They develop attachments and dislikes over the coming weeks and months until the school year ends. When school begins anew, the cycle of introductions, attitudes, value judgments, and shifting loyalties repeats itself.

In contrast, scholars enter a one-room schoolhouse with a group of peers from their neighborhood, including those from their church and, often, members of their extended family. They know most (if not all) of these peers and their families before ever setting foot in the school. They will sit in a classroom housing first through eighth grades. There will be one teacher, also an eighth grade graduate.[4] If female, she will maintain authority over the classroom but will demonstrate submissive behavior in the presence of men, as appropriate. If male, he will also demonstrate submissive behavior in the presence of men above him in the hierarchy. If the school is large enough to require two teachers, the lower four grades will sit on one side of the room, with the upper four grades on the other. In these larger schools, during periods when separate lessons require a lecture or discussion, a curtain is often drawn across the middle of the room to create a modicum of privacy. Attachments and dislikes are baked into relationships long before scholars meet in this venue. While there will be an ebb and flow, they will largely remain together across eight years, in the same school and in the same classroom, with relatively little change, other than the teacher.[5] During unstructured times, such as recess, their play follows gender-appropriate activities.

Despite these expectations, teaching is an area where gender roles are changing. For many years, young single females taught in Amish schools not as a career, but as one of the few acceptable occupations until they married. Recently, salaries have increased. As a result, young males take an interest in the classroom. Unlike some tasks, this is not a case of males offering assistance in a female role. Instead, it is a traditional female role opening up to greater diversity. The long-term outcome of this expansion, which includes a longer tenure for some teachers, remains to be seen. One reason it may be tolerated is that the heteronormative status quo, supporting the patriarchy, is undisturbed. Despite this relative stability the economic impact does displace females, as males gravitate to what are now better-paying positions. This reduction in females employed within an Amish community encourages them to seek jobs in the larger workforce. While they remain in positions that are traditionally female or gender neutral, the unintended consequence is their greater autonomy and interaction with the world.

While many expectations for Amish males and females will be identical, there are distinctions, and teachers rigidly adhere to them. These expectations are embedded in the broader hierarchy of roles, with teachers at the top and the scholars' influence descending by grade.

Upper grades model appropriate behaviors for lower grades and, at times, assist with assignments or activities. Once again, it is not age per se, but wisdom gained by that age and maturity, that gives older peers this status.

The intertwining of patriarchal and female authority advances in a structured manner during these youths' years as scholars. Whether they attend an Amish school or spend time in a public school, these children are often exposed to female authority. Within the home, a mother, as well as grandmothers, aunts, and even older sisters, have wielded power. In that venue, however, males have been present as a buttress or an ultimate authoritarian presence. In the classroom, a female teacher has immediate and primary control. In Amish schools, their authority is backstopped by a board, composed exclusively of men, but scholars do not observe this male presence on a day-to-day basis. They see women working in a venue in which their authority is primary.

Upon graduation from the eighth grade, there is a liminal period in which an adolescent is no longer a scholar but is still too young to embark on Rumspringa. Females use this time to refine their skills as homemakers. Males often take on an informal apprentice role, either with an extended family member or in the home. Childhood is being packed away, and, with it, the tolerance for play and immature amusements. The parameters of distinct gender roles continue to crystallize, based on family, church, and settlement expectations. These will drive the vocational choices available to Amish adolescents, as well as establish their places in the social hierarchy. While still relying heavily on those who are older for wisdom, these young people are gaining both practical and academic knowledge bases of their own, providing them with greater status. They remain on the lower rungs of the hierarchical ladder, but they have stepped above the powerless position of a child.

Loosening the Reins: Rumspringa

Rumspringa gives the appearance of the Amish developmental stage that divests itself from cultural control. The skewed and histrionic lens of mainstream media portrays it as a time of unbridled debauchery, with parents wringing their hands in helpless frustration. But the reality is not as extreme for participants, or their parents, as the hype suggests.

Rumspringa (loosely translated as "running around") often begins on one's sixteenth birthday. Among its multiple purposes, this period gives a youth raised in an Amish family the opportunity to date and find a marriage partner,[6] particularly for those already firm in their commitment to join the church. For those who hold lingering doubts as to whether they wish to remain Amish for the rest of their lives, it also gives them the freedom to make a deliberate and voluntary choice to join the church or to separate from it.[7] For this latter group, the options sound stark and polarized. Again, the trumped-up image is akin to the reality show where vanloads of Amish sixteen-year-olds were dumped on a street corner in New York City with a suitcase and a wad of cash, encouraged to return only if they made the appropriate choice. In actual practice, few leave their communities, or even their homes, during Rumspringa. The extent of their emotional separation falls on a continuum, suggesting that even maintaining a distance from Amish culture is mitigated by the social hierarchy.

First, there is the length of time a youth spends in Rumspringa. Settlements on the progressive end of the spectrum witness a developmental stage that can last, in some of the more anxiety-provoking cases, into one's early twenties. Conservative communities exert pressure for this stage to end in a few months, or a year at most.[8] Therefore, while this is a period of voluntary contemplation, the cultural clock ticks loudly.

A second factor is the lifestyle in which a youth engages during this time. Some communities turn a blind eye while males (and, more recently in some settlements, females) purchase and drive motor vehicles. Some tolerate English clothes, which again is more often a male fashion statement, at least at home.[9] Many smoke cigarettes, and a number binge drink on weekends. Some also use marijuana and, to a lesser extent, other drugs.

Third, residence has an influence. The majority of parents, while deeply unhappy when their adolescent acts out, tolerate a surprising dose of "wild child" behavior so their son or daughter will continue to live at home. The logic is pragmatic. A child still surrounded by the influence of an Amish lifestyle also remains more restrained than would otherwise be true. Those in this situation are more likely to return to the fold than if their parents impart rigid, nonnegotiable rules and force them to live elsewhere, away from the nurture and modeling, as well as the pressure, that home provides.

Fourth, few in Rumspringa distance themselves from their culture. They act out, but they do so in concert with other Amish. The term "Driving While Amish" was coined in the Elkhart-LaGrange settlement, due to the frequency with which law enforcement stops carloads of underage Amish either in possession of or consuming alcohol.[10] The tendency for Amish peers to act out together yet remain engaged in more innocuous group behaviors, such as Sunday singings, continues across this period.

Fifth, Rumspringa is the culturally sanctioned opportunity to interact with the opposite gender with a minimum of parental supervision. Singings occur at home, so parents are in the background, but participants often engage without a watchful adult eye. This is also a period for dating, as the search for a life partner begins in earnest.

Amish culture therefore continues to exert a significant influence during this tempestuous time. Still, even those who have every intention of remaining within the Amish fold see this as their last hurrah before resigning themselves to the Ordnung that will be theirs to follow upon joining the church and marrying, decisions that bring this phase of life to a close. For those who walk away from the church, the culture still maintains a subtle influence. While not required, there is greater satisfaction for the family if these malcontents settle into a similar church discipline, which can include, but is not limited to, a Mennonite congregation. The pressure to do so from family and friends who remain in the Amish church is a control that reminds even a child who leaves that their culture's imprint is indelible for anyone raised in its grasp.

Sexual behavior during Rumspringa varies, correlated with a youth's willingness to step away from the morality of the community. Predictably, the use of alcohol and other drugs accompanies this sexual freedom, and casual sexual encounters are more common among participants who imbibe heavily. And yet, all have been raised in Amish families, churches, and settlements. Across the span of their short but inquisitive lives, they have seen their foreordained future modeled in the Amish church: baptism, marriage for life, children, hard work, and an unyielding commitment to God and community. For many, Rumspringa is a hedonistic opportunity they will not have again, and sexual freedom is an unabashed element in that adventure. Those youth who are more sedate or conservative will quickly begin courting and search for a life partner, but even here the potential for sexual acting out remains.

The expectations for dating and sexual activity in Rumspringa hearken back to earlier twentieth-century America. The assumption exists that if females impose limits on sex, men will accept these limits, a belief that spanned the 1920s through the 1950s in some form.[11] In tame groups, or gangs, such virtuous behavior is perceived as noble. In wilder gangs, the same behavior ensures a lack of popularity, compared with females willing to engage in a wider range of sexual behavior. Male attitudes will often reverse post-Rumspringa, when a desirable wife is one who has been chaste.

Sexual control in Rumspringa is therefore often perceived as the responsibility of the female. In the heteronormative espoused by the Amish culture, young males are hormonally driven and excused for their desire to be indiscrete. Females reverse roles and become the dominant gender, acting as gatekeepers, limiting sexual activity, and ensuring that rules are followed.[12] This attitude rationalizes the excesses of these younger patriarchal members. It also models yet another situation in which females are empowered and supersede males, but exercising this power can come at the cost of their popularity, at least in some gangs.

Rumspringa loosens the reins of cultural control. Forms of acting out that would be censored if committed by fully invested members are tolerated. The culture manages this developmental phase by redefining heteronormative expectations, so that controls remain but are pragmatically adjusted. Behaviors that violate moral norms still fall under the rubric of acting out. The fact that there are no tangible consequences does not excuse them. A Rumspringa participant has a clear understanding that these are behaviors that will either be relinquished or confessed if they continue after joining the church. Acting out during Rumspringa occurs within the context of the collective society, is understood to be time limited, and will ultimately result in a shamefaced renunciation of the phase. It then becomes clear that Rumspringa participants never actually leave the culture. The majority will turn away from these excesses and formally embrace the church that allowed this brief freedom.

Submitting Again: Church Membership

The transition into Rumspringa is abrupt, a sprint that begins at the sixteen-year-old age marker. The changeover out of this period gives the impression that it is equally abrupt, ending with the baptism that marks church membership. (Rumspringa formally ends with marriage.)[13] Yet this rarely occurs. A decision to join the church signals an intent to abandon hedonistic pursuits, but such pleasures, once experienced, are not easily laid aside. Late adolescents and young adults who engage in alcohol-fueled parties and raucous singings often continue in their wicked ways after baptism. These include sexual acting out, but with a fundamental difference.

They have now become members of the church and, as such, should be guided by the Ordnung. Still, clergy are parents and former adolescents themselves. They recall their own struggles as the novitiate members attempt to forego the temptations of Rumspringa. Accordingly, these young adults are often granted a grace period, neither defined nor formally recognized, that tolerates acting out. This forbearance may overlook inappropriate behaviors, provide warnings without consequences, or expect informal acknowledgement of transgressions in situations that would demand formal confession from a more mature church member. However acting out is handled, new members can face a gentle slope, as opposed to a steep gradient of discipline, as they are guided into the fold.

Despite this lingering tolerance, new church members are rapidly exposed to previously inaccessible aspects of community life. They now are participants in semiannual communion, the most sacred covenant in the Amish church.[14] Communion is restricted to members and anticipates that animosities, disagreements, or any lack of fellowship will be resolved prior to sharing this symbolic meal. The service is a reminder in multiple ways. It recalls the expectation of the collective culture that members share a common goal—the mission of the Christian church. It is an act that symbolizes the agonizing transition from Jesus's earthly ministry to a glorious and transcendent rule. It binds members in recalling the death of their Savior, a sacrifice for the very sins, including sexual sins, that led God to send his Son to earth. In a much more pragmatic way, it reminds members of the deep and abiding bond they share with one another, as believers and as Amish. It is a hallmark of the social and theological forces that contribute to the collective intimacy of Amish life.

At its best, communion is a moment of epiphany, celebrating the assembled church and its common mission. These neophyte members also participate in the rite of confession, a time that reminds the assembled church of the need to stay faithful to that common mission. They observe the confession of fellow members who have strayed, and they can be called to account for themselves. They are expected to confess voluntarily if their conscience moves them. The collective culture encircles and tightens its bonds as church membership draws them more fully into the life of the community.

There is no formula for leaving Rumspringa and keeping it as a distant memory (one, moreover, that is hopefully forgotten as mem-

bers focus on finding purity in their lives). For those who have joined
the church but are not yet prepared for marriage, it fades as dating
becomes an earnest search for a life partner. Ironically, sexual intimacy
to the point of intercourse is now less common, at least in the early
stages of courtship, as the watchful eye of the community focuses more
closely on any serious couple than was true during the more-tolerant
period prior to church membership.

Consistent with tradition, a male is responsible for proposing to a
female, but a female retains the right to refuse. The onus of remaining unmarried is equally applied to both sexes,[15] although males are
better positioned financially if they are single. The decision to join
the church and marry is an overt recognition of the patriarchy and
an agreement by each gender to abide by the rules of male dominance
and female submission. Men understand that they are taking on a role
in a patriarchy and a hierarchy that can elevate their status if selected
as clergy members, or can leave them much where they are, except
for the demands of family. Women comprehend that theirs will be
the role of matriarch. Neither the Ordnung nor some churches stop
women from pursuing vocations and avocations, provided these do
not interfere with a female's primary role as wife and mother, but
neither do they support these efforts. It is with such expectations that
couples enter the next phase of their lives.

The Intertwined Hierarchy: Marriage and Leadership

There is a lingering, subtle attitude that a marriage partner should
bring attributes of financial stability and a strong work ethic to the
table.[16] Still, most of today's Amish young adults prefer (as do their
mainstream culture counterparts) to choose a life partner based on
romantic attraction. It would be naïve to suggest that Amish partners
have a full awareness of a potential mate's life. In comparison with
English partners, however, they gain an in-depth knowledge from
friends and confidantes that boggles the imagination. A collective,
high-context culture offers far fewer places to hide information.[17] Even
so, problems, as occur with all such data, include accuracy, skewed

perceptions by the reporter, a lack of context for at least some pieces of knowledge, and the all-too-human ability to still hide secrets, even in the most brightly lit places. Nevertheless, the information available on the partner and the partner's parents, grandparents, siblings, aunts, uncles, cousins, nieces, and nephews provides a comprehensive history normally lacking in mainstream relationships.

Once married, the couple do not whisk themselves away to start a new life. Instead, they continue to establish roles within extended family systems that are now blended, a process that began once a serious relationship became evident. Fresh responsibilities face this new nuclear family. The first is to produce children. Procreation is an expectation of marriage, and the extended family eagerly awaits birth announcements.

Second, the husband now has the potential to be chosen as a clergy member. Any married man in good standing within the church can be placed in consideration for becoming a deacon or a minister (and, from the ministers, for being chosen later as bishop if a vacancy arises). Election by lot draws mixed emotions. The position is lifelong, unless ill health obliges a resignation; there is no financial remuneration; responsibilities are at times overwhelming; and the position can have strong political overtones.[18] But a failure to be nominated is seen as an absence, a reminder that too few members believe one is qualified. Nomination and choice therefore produce a tense moment for the family. The narrow window of a best outcome may be to have the family patriarch nominated but not selected, a nod to the esteem bestowed by the church while avoiding the responsibilities being chosen would entail.

Despite the proliferation of gender-specific chores, many tasks are gender neutral. These may be assigned on the basis of age. Younger children are responsible for easily handled tasks. As they mature, they graduate to complex or demanding household chores, and younger siblings assume the simple jobs. In other cases, the best way to complete certain duties may be to find creative solutions. For example, one family universally hated polishing shoes. Accordingly, it was a chore that rotated weekly between members, lessening its frequency for all involved. Other duties, such as cutting hair, planting, harvesting, and milking, are tasks that cross gender boundaries on a regular basis.

The husband/father is the head of the household, a position of authority he maintains in several ways. The primary one is financial. Women may create and sell crafts and foodstuffs, or engage in similar part-time employment. They may be entrepreneurs, even publishing magazines.[19] Activities such as quilting allow them to act as businesswomen and support an identity separate from that of a homemaker.[20] Their work is considered supplementary to the work of a husband, however. He has ultimate authority in decisions that impact the family. Some couples consider the wife's input on major decisions to be essential, but a final choice could not be made without the husband's presence.

As more men have begun to work away from home,[21] greater responsibility and authority are thrust onto the role of wife. Thus the heteronormative ideal continues to evolve. The term "soft patriarch," coined by W. Bradford Wilcox,[22] applies, although with a different twist than its original meaning. The heteronormative in Amish culture is patriarchal, but equally, it is hierarchical. If the patriarchal primary authority is absent, a vacuum forms, which is filled by the next authority in line. In the home, females take on authoritarian roles. Inevitably, they are charged with decisions about the house, the farmette, the children, and daily life that cannot be deferred until the husband/father is available. The demands of this decision making lead to a parity in authority that favors women. Males continue to hold financial power in most families, so they are perceived as the ultimate decision makers, but a wide range of responsibilities can shift to females. Accordingly, the degree of female submission diminishes. (The church hierarchy has been less impacted by this change. As females remain excluded from the clergy, traditional heteronormative expectations hold sway.)

As an example of the outcome of this change in authority, an attorney in the Lancaster area has noted that when he does property and deed work, Amish wives are much more invested than non-Amish farm wives. He attributes the difference to an Amish wife's commitment to the farm itself, whereas non-Amish farm wives often have careers of their own.[23]

The parity of women also varies within and between Amish affiliations. Historically, the greater the level of interaction with the surrounding non-Amish community, the less egalitarian women's roles are in the settlement.[24] This is consistent with a heteronormative response to perceived pressure by the mainstream. To maintain power and control within the collective culture, greater submission is required for those who are most likely to be influenced by an alternative model. The female's role as submissive partner does not appear to create significant emotional distress, however. An empirical study supports the emotional and physical well-being of Amish women in comparison with non-Amish peers.[25]

Regardless of the struggles that occur in family life, the years pass, and there eventually comes a day when the last child leaves and the couple is alone once again. This phase marks the sunset of their time together and signals another shift in the balance of power.

Out the Other Side: Empty Nest, Dawdi, and Mommi

Dawdi and *mommi* are dialect terms for "grandfather" and "grandmother." As children mature, join the church, and begin families of their own, the physical limitations of aging parents become a need to be addressed. Eventually the couple may move to a dawdyhaus, a smaller dwelling built specifically for older parents next to a family home. It allows these elders to live independently, but with the support and, if necessary, supervised care of family members.

The elderly are respected in Amish culture and continue to fulfill important roles within family and church. As they age, the emphasis moves to gleaning knowledge from accumulated wisdom as their physical health declines. Their authority in the collective culture varies. If the husband is a clergy member, he retains much of his power, provided he can perform the necessary duties. If he is relegated to inactive clergy, his role within the church and the family diminishes. For example, a bishop and his wife built a dawdyhaus next to an adult son and his wife. Initially, as their health was good and they maintained their independence, the relationship was one of equals. Over time, they faced health problems common to aging, as well as accompanying health crises. While the couple continued as respected elders, the demands related to their care and their weakened physical capacity gradually shifted the relationship. The caretaking role consumed more of their children's time, and the parents became more physically dependent. While still respected and loved, the elderly couple's roles as patriarch and matriarch of the family gradually slipped away.

Power and control are concentrated in the most productive members of society, as is true in most cultures, but the Amish heteronormative anticipates caretaking for elders. While their authority in the community may be diminished, they are a part of its history. Just as all aspects of the culture's history are respected, so, too, are these older Amish. While the elderly continue the gender roles stamped into place across the course of a lifetime, the vocational and parenting demands that so clearly define these roles for younger adults recede. There is often an even greater, albeit unspoken, egalitarian status between older men and women.

The soft patriarchy of Amish life is one that anticipates the submission of women. Yet that submission is neither inflexible nor consistent. Women experience a rich, complex, and variable level of inequality with their dominant counterparts. These interactions adapt and accommodate across a lifespan and within circumstances, so women can achieve a parity, particularly in the family system, that is not immediately apparent. These roles and the interactions they require in a collective and high-context culture demand an intimacy that differs from that of the mainstream. This experience is the subject of the next chapter.

Chapter Six

Intimacy

The True Serpent in the Garden

Having been befriended by several Amish families, I have a vantage point from which to compare changes as our ages settle into the upper half of double digits. For all, houses empty as our children take on lives of their own. We become grandparents (and, for some Amish friends, great-grandparents). We experience the joys and sorrows adult children bring, now physically separate but still in our sphere of influence. I catch available moments with my busy offspring as we try to coordinate schedules for a meal or a quick cup of coffee. Keeping up with nieces and nephews means using Facebook and text messages, as our sincere promises to connect in person are rarely fulfilled. With my parents' generation gone, I exchange Christmas cards, my sole communication, with cousins flung across the country. My friends are intimates, closer than family. And stacking these relationships against Amish peers? There, couples who once had seven, eight, even ten or more kids under their roof now live as empty nesters. But they are visited daily by a complement of children, in-laws, and grandchildren. They, in turn, are in frequent contact with their parents, aunts, uncles, and siblings. They meet with neighbors and regularly attend their own and other churches. They are rarely alone. Their time is filled with work and socializing. Intimacy for me is moments caught in the intersecting whirl of busy schedules. Intimacy for them? In a collective culture it is the ebb and flow of interactions with those many persons who compose their daily lives. Indeed, how we conceptualize intimacy is radically different.

"Now the serpent was more subtil than any beast of the field which the Lord God had made. . . . Then the Lord God said, Behold, the man is become as one of us, to know good and evil" (Genesis 3:1a, 22a, KJV). These verses bookend a story of deceit and betrayal for the first couple. The serpent convinces Eve that she deserves knowledge that had been forbidden to humankind. Dire consequences follow for her, for Adam, and for all generations. If the story is taken literally, as the Amish do, this selfish act spills evil into the world. If the story is apocryphal, the serpent can be seen as symbolic of the deep and unmet need that abides in each of us, the desire to be known and understood, and the simultaneous fear that others may know us too well. That universal struggle, symbolized by the serpent, leaves us vulnerable, longing, hopeful, and dismayed.

Over time this visceral longing is tempered by the shelter of a culture that offers security and support.[1] At its best, intimacy transcends the expectation that others pay attention to us. We surmount egocentric needs and experience the deep contentment of emotional sharing. Still, the rich complexity of intimate expression, and the purposes for which it is employed, crystallize within the context of culture.

This chapter explores intimacy as expressed within the Amish heteronormative. It creates cohesion within the family, church, and settlement, powerful bonds that ensure the primacy of Amish beliefs. It simultaneously limits the strength, duration, and constancy of relationships with those who are not Amish, a permeable interpersonal barrier that nevertheless forbids full entry into this tight-knit fellowship. Queering intimacy, that ephemeral but integral social construct,[2] is essential to understand the dynamics of this Plain people.

Defining Intimacy for the Amish

Repeated use of terms such as "high-context" and "collective" runs the risk of creating labels instead of a convenient shorthand for dynamic concepts. Amish culture, which is high context and collective, is the outgrowth of a spiritual purpose. That purpose is embodied in *Gelassenheit*. The term encompasses the views of late-medieval

Anabaptists, who advocated an unconditional surrender to the will of their Savior. For martyrs to their cause, it meant a literal choice to abandon their bodies to God.[3] In the present day, it reflects a decision to subsume individual will and freedom to the greater good, and to yield to the authority of the church. Members sacrifice self-interest to the well-being of the community.

Paul Kline, a New Order Amish deacon, has written a treatise on Gelassenheit.[4] His comments apply globally to the Amish. In the preamble, he defines its relationship to love:

> The church's calling is to give this principle bodily form in everyday life. The object of Gelassenheit is a loving brotherhood or the kingdom of God here on earth. The church is the visible body of Christ on earth. As Christ suffered and died, so His followers are called to suffer and die to self. Christ's great love refused to use force to gather people into His kingdom. We need to live through the same process of redemption by surrendering our self-will and freeing ourselves from all arrogance and assertiveness. We believe that in this way the power of God's love will create a brotherhood in Christ.

Analyses by Amish scholars discuss a culture founded on mutual love and trust. John Hostetler says, "The Amish are in some ways a little commonwealth, for their members claim to be ruled by the law of love and redemption."[5] Support is grounded in communal rules, as noted in a more recent book, *The Amish*: "The theme of obedience undergirds the entire socioreligious system by fusing faith with life, and the individual with the community. . . . The emphasis on discipleship and obedience means that Amish faith focuses more on *how* one lives than on *what* one believes."[6]

Intimacy is respect for other persons, submission to the anticipated rules (Ordnung), and an attitude of self-sacrifice in which the needs of the other come first. This construct differs from intimacy between two people, or even between members of a family. This is intimacy with an entire group, as barriers are swept away by an expectation of self-surrender. *The Amish* describes the Pennsylvania Dutch terms *uffgewe* (to give up) and *unnergewe* (to give under) as essential elements of the relationship between individual and community.[7] Each person sacrifices (gives up) and yields (gives under) to the whole.

Such self-surrender and mutual care underlie a collective and high-context culture.[8] Because actions are predicated on their impact for the larger group, the most limited interpersonal interactions impinge at multiple levels. Even information about utterly casual exchanges can expand exponentially, much like throwing a pebble into a quiet pond. As it breaks the surface, ripples spread in all directions. Long after the pebble is submerged and lost to view, these ripples serve as a reminder of its presence.

This contrasts with low-context postmodern culture, in which interactions between individuals or even groups are given limited breadth within the context of of social knowledge. One of our salient values is autonomy, fostering individual achievement and competition.[9] This desire for autonomy makes information a valuable commodity to withhold. For example, we might interact with our clergy, the contractor working on our home, a good friend, and our neighbor during a day, all of them people with whom we have discrete, clearly defined, and limited relationships. To maintain our status as autonomous individuals, we would not choose to tell our contractor about our spiritual battles, or our clergy about our dalliance with another person's spouse. Among the Amish it would not be unusual for a man to meet and share all that was occurring in his life with his minister, the contractor working on his home, a good friend, and his neighbor, since the same individual assumes all of these roles! Not only would an Amish neighbor be privy to these personal aspects of another member's life, but he would also know about similar struggles in the extended family. In a competitive culture, emphasizing individual achievement, such sharing would not encourage intimacy, but instead would be destructive. In a collective culture, emphasizing common goals, such sharing strengthens bonds.[10]

By definition, then, intimacy in a collective society is more inclusive. We speak of the strong and cohesive nature of the collective, but how are these relationships explained psychologically? Beginning as a toddler, an essential developmental task is the recognition of "me" and "not me," the ability to separate what is the child from what is *not* the child.[11] From this humble beginning emerges a complex sense of self, or identity. In mainstream culture, a personal identity, or "me," takes on meaning by sharing values with subcultures but placing one's ultimate value on a unique sense of self. For the Amish, this "me" assumes meaning not only by sharing values, but also by melding seamlessly with the surrounding culture. A unique sense of self is present, but it is subdued by a recognition that it is secondary to service to the whole. Individuals unable to adapt to this collective identification struggle to find a place among the Amish.[12]

A broad-based intimacy serves several purposes. First, it ensures the cohesion of the group, necessary for the efficacy of a collective. Second, it creates a natural boundary. The Amish experience a closeness with other Plain people that is not replicated with those of the world, tamping down the desire to stray. Third, it reinforces obedience, including to the heteronormative, as members of the culture remain emotionally dependent on each other. That interdependence buttresses a desire to please. Fourth, it enforces the system of authority, another aspect of the heteronormative. Power and control remain vested in the patriarchy, who oversee community well-being.

The role of romance and the qualities males and females seek in a mate have been addressed in other writings about the Amish, but primarily to mention that romance is downplayed, while other attributes of a spouse have greater importance.[13] This chapter amplifies these explorations, as well as in-depth emotional relationships of other types.

Reconfiguring Intimacy

Collective intimacy complicates a dyadic relationship. It is identical in many respects and, in others, parallels the paradigm in mainstream culture. Amish individuals who anticipate emotional closeness, even in friendship, must first share values, core beliefs, pragmatic guidelines for daily behavior, and aspirational guidelines for the spiritual journey.[14] These values are manifested by other Plain people, who also embrace expectations of sacrificial living. Their values inherently coincide. Plain groups sacrifice the ease of postmodern life to create a more cohesive Christian community. Overlapping mutual values exist with those outside the Amish fold, but explorations there are tentative, and relationships are developed with caution. These can also be fragile, and the influence of family and church often means that they will be transitory.

Mutual respect engenders a reciprocal regard, but the power of the collective creates a different definition of respect than the one we assume. In mainstream culture, where autonomy is paramount, intimacy is a process of establishing parameters, acknowledging preferences, and discovering key areas of disagreement, where the intensity of these disagreements is part of that process. In a collective culture, the same process occurs, but in far more muted tones. There is greater emphasis on minimizing parameters, finding mutual preferences, and downplaying disagreements. This is a manifestation of the deeply ingrained emphasis on self-surrender.

The Amish also advocate humility. It addresses pride and anticipates that the individual will avoid calling attention to self in preference to the community.[15] Interpersonal interactions that are humble maintain dignity and respect for all involved. Beyond the parameters of the Ordnung, however, there are no limitations on relationships. Personal freedom allows self-expression in friendships and with romantic partners. Yet family, friends, and clergy can and do offer their opinions on the merits of a friendship or a romantic choice, as is true in any culture.

Shared values and mutual respect are the bedrock of intimacy, but simply being Amish does not guarantee universal reciprocal values. It bears repeating that the concept "the" Amish does not exist. Instead, it refers to a number of affiliations.[16] Nor is it simply a matter of giving assent to the church's Ordnung. It also includes the stringency with which the Ordnung is enforced, a rigor that also varies. Each of these dynamics is a reciprocal process, as an individual or a family must make decisions about the transparency of a relationship based on the acceptance of the church. Less well-accepted relationships face a greater challenge.

Romantic relationships, for example, can generate tension if the partners are from churches that are not in fellowship or interpret fidelity to the Ordnung differently. This situation can happen even in Amish churches of the same affiliation.[17] Differences in the interpretation of general rules, the handling of a case of excommunication, or shunning, or of alliances in church disputes are the most common reasons for one church to withdraw from fellowship with another. It does not mean that two persons from churches that disagree are prohibited from romantic involvement, but there is a discomfort surrounding their relationship that would not otherwise be present.

Assuming that a relationship passes the tests of mutual values, respect, and belonging, the next step is an increasing trust. Amish culture is not only collective, but also hierarchical, and, as such, power and control are interwoven into all aspects of life. As with any culture, it is advantageous to stay in the good graces of those in power. In a collective and high-context culture, knowledge of transgressions easily finds its way to the clergy. And, as with any culture with a broad and scrupulous set of expectations, all individuals make choices about the rules they follow diligently and those they relax. In such an atmosphere, trust is a significant consideration in meaningful sharing. As the emotional dominoes fall, there may ultimately come not just a sense of liking for the other person, not just a genuine affection, but also a deeper emotion. Be it filial or romantic, love is the end result of these dynamic stages.

It is a relative rarity for empirical literature to generalize to an Amish population, but in this case a psychological construct does. A longstanding awareness, based on evidence from multiple studies, is that religion is a source of marital stability.[18] The sanctification of the marriage bond facilitates the perceived quality of a marital relationship. Research supports this finding in several ways. Newlyweds report greater satisfaction,[19] as do those transitioning into parenthood.[20] Married individuals also report a greater sense of well-being,[21] as well as a stronger attachment.[22] Trust and love, the end results of the proposed trajectory, occur within the context of a highly religious society among the Amish.

Still, several caveats attend this empirical finding. First, it applies to emotions. Rarely, if ever, do humans proceed in calculated, rational, and logical steps with regard to emotional issues. Therefore, the trajectory of stability in a marriage is apt to be marked by stops and starts, detours, and reversals. Second, social scientists have come late to the party to explain romantic love, an effort the literati have more eloquently embraced for thousands of years. For those who live out the fairytale, falling madly in love and forsaking all other considerations in pursuit of their quest, this book does not attempt to add to the myriad explanations linking head and heart (although jaded social scientists refer to this phase as "infatuation"). Suffice to say, the model suggested is insufficient, as are they all, to explain the vagaries where "there are strings in the human heart that had better not be vibrated."[23]

The weak spots in the fortification of the Amish heteronormative are demonstrated in the *process* of intimacy. Barriers erected by the culture and the Ordnung can be carefully crafted and set in place. Participants in that culture can be raised from childhood with these expectations, and the emphases on similar values and membership in a collective are difficult to challenge. But when these "strings in the human heart" vibrate and emotional choices outweigh the intellectual ones, all of these boundaries can be for naught. The patriarchy can only hope that the lessons of discipline, obedience, and Gelassenheit are sufficient to guide emotional needs.

How does intimacy play out? The following sections examine close relationships in various arenas of Amish life.

Familial Intimacy

Comedian George Burns quipped, "Happiness is having a loving, close-knit family—in another city." The Amish would disagree with

Burns's criterion for happiness. The network of relationships that composes the system is indispensable to their social network. A camaraderie exists in the extended family that is difficult to understand for those outside a collective culture. Yet this intimacy does not imply an equal closeness for all. As with any group, there are degrees. Still, there is an expectation for unity, understanding, and support because of the familial bond. That support will ebb and flow, as does the level of intimacy. Tensions and conflict are inherent in interpersonal relationships. Their culture may be collective and high context, but that does not immunize the Amish against these struggles. Busied with the demands of daily life, there is neither time nor, in some cases, the inclination to resolve each of the disagreements and squabbles that arise. As a result, "in-laws" and "out-laws" appear in abundance. (These tensions do tend to be put aside in the face of family crises, as happens in any culture.)

In a hierarchical society such as that of the Amish, the resolution of disputes often evolves in a structured manner. Decision making defers at least nominally to men, and the opinions of older men or clergy bear more weight than those of younger males. The reality is more intertwined as women covertly or even overtly sway the opinions of patriarchs. Regardless of their influence, this input is usually offered in a discrete manner, so the ultimate decision is projected from male authority. The heteronormative does not permit the power of the patriarchy to be relinquished, at least in the foreground.

Family intimacy is likely to be prominently on display at two times: in moments of crisis, and in response to the needs of aging parents. A crisis may be medical, emotional, or financial. Regardless, immediate and extended family are aware and offer help. This includes practical needs, such as assisting with chores, childcare, and responsibilities in the home. It can also include offering moral support, such as visiting a person who is in a hospital or recuperating at home, or sending cards and letters. For example, an expectant mother gave birth in a local hospital to a child with a life-threatening medical issue. The newborn was airlifted to a facility with a wider range of services.

The child's grandfather rode in the helicopter with the father, while approximately eight relatives from both sides of the family followed by van, in order to be present as soon as possible for support. Such a scenario is not uncommon.

The needs of aging parents also require conjoint decision making. If parents are infirm but still able to live independently, choosing the child on whose property to build a dawdyhaus is decided between the siblings. Likewise, there is often discussion and consensus on payment for materials, the building process, and a timeline for completion. If a parent becomes too enfeebled to live alone, children rotate the responsibility of providing housing, again a decision reached by consensus. The expectation that parents will be offered care by their children and remain in the community, rather than being placed in a nursing facility, increases the demand for communication and interaction, hence intimacy, between family members. A similar scenario plays out if a sibling is disabled.

With approximately seven children per family, it is inevitable that some of the siblings will have closer bonds. There is often a protective element to these relationships if one sibling is older. In mainstream culture, siblings might choose to work together, but their historical inequality can cause frequent tension. Many drift apart in adulthood, and what were once inequalities become rivalries that emerge intermittently during holiday visits. For the Amish, many siblings continue to be involved across their lifetimes, either employed together in non-Amish construction or factories, or cooperating in joint business ventures. The dynamics first learned in childhood continue, supported by the hierarchy of the culture. As both business associates and siblings, there can be an inequity in the relationship that fans resentments, but these are subsumed under collective expectations.[24]

At times, a disparity reverses. If a younger sibling becomes a member of the clergy, his status elevates him over that of older siblings. Tensions and resentments flip-flop as the family adjusts to this change. Or two siblings may be chosen as clergy in different Gmays. If this occurs, their relationship can have conflicts if the Ordnungs of their churches clash and they fail to find common ground. An example of the latter involves two brothers who were extremely close until each was elevated to bishop. Living across the road from one another, but leading separate churches, they fell into disagreement over a rule. Their churches were no longer in fellowship, and they rarely spoke until the younger bishop was dying. From his deathbed, he asked forgiveness from his brother for the longstanding feud.

Family and friends are thus an essential element of intimacy among the Amish, although the manner in which that intimacy plays out is bounded by the hierarchical nature of the culture.

Marital Intimacy

With an uptick in cohabitation and the frequency of divorce, the mainstream is rapidly disillusioned with the idea that marriage is a lifetime commitment. For those who do make that prolonged investment, intimacy in a relationship that is anticipated to span forty, fifty, sixty, or more years includes, by its nature, an ebb and flow. A couple can find themselves buffeted not only by the natural transitions in their lifespan, but by temporal circumstances and crises that attend every journey.

For the Amish, marriage remains sacrosanct, the cornerstone of the family. As such, partners are expected to communicate, compromise on, and tolerate behaviors that might be viewed askance in the mainstream. The church serves as a mediator when needed. For example, if an issue of domestic violence arises, non-Amish clergy may side with the abused wife, arguing against violence in a relationship. Alternatively, fundamental Amish clergy may declare that just as Jesus suffered, so we suffer in this life in anticipation of a hoped-for reward in heaven. Therefore, while not supporting the fairness or validity of an abused wife's treatment, they argue for tolerance for the patriarch's behavior, protecting the heteronormative. There are rare occasions when couples are allowed by their bishop to separate, usually in response to unremitting domestic violence by the husband. This occurs only after prolonged efforts to resolve their differences, and these bishops form a scant minority. Even so, the couple remains married, as divorce is not an option.[25]

This example, which may be unsettling for some, demonstrates a primary difference in marital intimacy between Amish culture and that of the mainstream. Amish intimacy between romantic partners is predicated as the opposite of our postmodern culture. For the Amish, a lasting relationship creates a forum in which the couple will grow together. For the mainstream, the basis for longevity in a marriage is the couple's joint ability to grow and mature. This differing perspective indicates the reason for opposing attitudes toward divorce. If the relationship is a forum for growth (the Amish view), then leaving it sabotages the potential for change. Alternatively, if two people cannot grow together (the English view), there is no purpose in forcing them to remain in the relationship.

An Amish marriage is also more open than the postmodern experience, although not as this word is commonly used. Again, because it occurs in a high-context, collective culture, extended family and the church have a window into the alliance that the mainstream would find intrusive and offensive. While this does not lessen intimacy for the couple, it does create a more transparent relationship.

Although Amish women can be subjugated, as the response to domestic violence suggests, they can also hold authority in the marriage, as discussed in the previous chapter. In one instance, an Amish husband and father injured his arm badly with a saw, requiring surgery to reattach tendons. When I visited them, his wife shared that after the procedure, since his arm was still numb from the anesthesia, he intended to mend a fence. He also planned return to work as soon as possible, despite the physician's instructions that he stay home for several weeks. "I told him absolutely not," she said, facing him as she did so. "She did," he added, "and I can't believe she's making me sit at home until this heals!" The wife acted as a surrogate authority for the physician, ensuring that her husband followed medical expectations for healing. In some marriages he would have ignored her demands and pursued his work regardless. In this case he acceded to her will.

Church Intimacy

Complete more than a cursory tour of an Amish settlement, and "bench wagons" will be seen parked alongside barns and outbuildings. These are the vehicles used to move the benches and hymnals from house to house as families in each church rotate responsibility for the biweekly service. With an average of twenty to forty families in membership,[26] this duty usually falls to a household once or twice per year. The wagon signals that church has either recently been held in that home or soon will be. It also symbolizes a flurry of preparation, as the family cleans, mends, repairs, and anticipates the three-hour service and meal to follow. An Amish service creates an intimacy that is difficult to grasp for those whose worship is predicated on assembly in a structure specifically designed for that purpose.

The melding of church and home weaves the power and control of the hierarchy and the intimacy of the collective into a single strand. Bishop and ministers wield their influence as they rotate from home to home. They preach the word of God, exhorting the people to live Christian lives. They mete out discipline as appropriate, maintaining the church's proper relationship with God. Each home is available for inspection by neighbors and fellow church members, affirming that the rules for a household are scrupulously followed. Ministers are humbled by their presence in the community, not raised to a place of honor on a dais and behind a pulpit. While they are in authority, they also remain a part of the same people they control. Geographically and in the church setting, these are neighbors and fellow sojourners. Power is a delicate balance that tips first one way, and then the other, but remains on a scale known to all present.

Intimacy within the Christian church is expected to be spiritual. For mainstream Christians, the definition of spirituality may differ from that for Plain people. Mainstream Christians more often define "spiritual" as an emotional, charismatic experience.[27] For the Amish, such spirituality smacks of evangelism, a thrust they avoid.[28] Instead, spirituality is imbued with pragmatic undertones, as they acknowledge the need for their actions in daily life to model the Christian path.

Spirituality incorporates an awareness that the temporal equates with temporary and reflects fleeting moments on earth. The anticipated, hoped-for passage to an eternity with God is the ultimate purpose of life. The church supports this by creating a fellowship of like-minded believers who provide guidance. While their control over one's life is not absolute, their opinion holds powerful sway over one's actions and attitudes.

For example, prior to the semiannual rite of communion, church members must align themselves spiritually. Conflicts must be forgiven and resolved. At times churches will delay the sacrament, but more often members make peace with each other to create a spirit of unity. This demonstrates the power of cultural expectations to establish intimacy between persons who may not otherwise view themselves in a close relationship with each other. In the same way, individuals submit themselves to the humiliation of church discipline to garner its support. Media portrays a stern excommunication and the shunning of those who have either walked away from their Amish heritage or been forced out. In reality, most quietly chafe under church discipline or accept it as their due in the spirit of Gelassenheit. In either case, they are relieved to find themselves forgiven and restored, as opposed to leaving the church of their childhood.

As the church consists of a geographic district, it is not just worship on Sundays that creates this intimacy. It is daily life, living as neighbors with those who make up the church. It is shared events that occur between those in close proximity. It is children being sent to the same school, since schools often draw from the same church. It is a tight, collective culture, whose members' lives intertwine and are necessarily intimate in the ways in which they intersect and interact. For the church, it is an assurance that spiritual nurture and intimacy are one.

Cultural Intimacy, Within and Without

Ultimately, there is a bond between the Amish, a sense of belonging that transcends geographic or personal distance. Groups of Amish travelers will chat in restaurants and train stations, merely because each recognizes the other as fellow Plain people. The culture itself creates an intimacy, an awareness that their chosen lifestyle is misunderstood, as it is far different from the choice of the majority. The simple act of being Amish creates intimacy with others who share a similar heritage. The same cannot be said for relationships that cross the line into mainstream culture. These are friendships more likely to be constricted, bound by significant limitations.[29] If they do reach intimate depths, they tend to be marked by ambivalence as the Amish confidante struggles with the meaning of such closeness with an English friend.

The problems raised by a close-knit friendship outside the Amish are simple but profound. Within the collective culture, friendships are mutually bound by an Ordnung. It may not be the same Ordnung, and at times a clash of rules creates conflict, but even if friends are members of differing churches, the underlying spirit of the rules will be similar. The culture, both temporal and spiritual, has power and control over the relationship. Both parties are aware of, and agree to abide by these expectations.

As Amish draw closer to non-Amish, the former are still expected to live by their own rules. Non-Amish friends experience no such boundaries. They model a lifestyle free of the power and control of a collective culture. Ultimately, then, difficult decisions about exposing oneself to situations that violate the rules become more complex.[30] The better choice, in terms of staying within cultural confines, is to limit relationships with those who are not Amish.

That is also the logic behind the distance required for those who are excommunicated. The purpose of shunning is explicitly stated as being a loving reminder to the sinner that behaviors violating the rules of the church cannot be tolerated. Forgiveness follows a demonstration of repentance. Shunning also serves as a potent reminder to those who remain that there is a gulf between the Amish and the world, so that those whose behaviors distance them from the church cannot as easily imbue remaining members with worldly ideas.

The boundaries between the Amish and the world remain highly permeable, despite these restrictions. Without that ease of communication, they would be a cult. Friends remain a choice for each member of the church, whether Amish, former Amish, or English. The easiest, most accepted, and most intimate relationships will be within the group. Among the Amish, intimacy is based on loyalty. Within that group, one finds family, close friends, and a marriage partner. The intimacy experienced is rewarded with a tightly bound community that offers unfailing support across one's lifespan. In turn, an individual must remain within the culture's boundaries and expectations. That loyalty is a comfort and a much needed support in times of crisis. It creates a far-reaching intimacy, a sense of oneness and sustenance that cannot be replicated in the mainstream heteronormative, where intimacy is predicated on individuation and autonomy.

Nonetheless, there is a darker side. In a culture that maintains a patriarchal hierarchy, women can find themselves facing subjection, as well as submission. An abusive or neglectful husband can be supported by the loyalty of a hierarchical system forced to choose between the ideal of paternal leadership, or the decision to discipline the mistreatment of one human being toward another. If the act of discipline threatens the heteronormative status quo and its power, then the mistreatment may go unpunished. Too often, these same social forces attempt to limit external involvement when punishment *is* deemed appropriate, instead administering justice from within the Amish church. By using the coercion of social norms, Unfriddah, confession, and the Bann, they avoid appealing to, or even permitting, law enforcement to exert its authority. In this way the heteronormative allows the patriarchy to retain control.

To return to the issue of intimacy outside the culture, such a pervasive Amish experience can impinge on those who fall further down the continuum, away from the collective pole. For these individuals who struggle with a need for autonomy in at least some aspects of their lives, English confidantes become a release, a vital link to share aspects of themselves they do not want known within their larger culture. At the same time, there is often an accompanying guilt for what feels like a betrayal of their values.

Intimacy is a powerful social force that binds Amish culture. At times it exists for good, and at others, it works to the detriment of individuals in its care.

Chapter Seven

Suffer Little Children

Child Sexual Abuse

Imagine a man pointing a gun within inches of a child and shooting. He does so without provocation, without even knowing who she is. He does so because she fits an agenda created in a deeply paranoid and distorted plan to exact a revenge that will never be understood. He takes his own life after repeating this action nine more times, murdering five of his innocent victims and irrevocably scarring the lives of the remaining girls and their families.

On October 2, 2006, Charles Roberts mercilessly gunned down ten Amish girls, ages six to thirteen, at the Nickel Mines School in the Lancaster, Pennsylvania, area.[1] The incident would have made global headlines for its brutal atrocity alone. But what stunned the world was the willingness of the Amish to forgive the perpetrator of this senseless act. In order to create sound bites that fit the terse style of modern journalism, the media truncated the process of grief. In place of what was a slow, onerous path, earnest reporters represented the Amish as capable of a neatly packaged spiritual resolution, not a messy emotional journey toward an ultimate effort to forgive. Still, the essence of the story was correct. They had set a foot on the road to forgiveness, determined to walk that path to the end.

In contrast to this externally imposed horror, imagine the situation where an Amish father awakens three of his daughters late at night. He takes them to the basement of the family home, places them in line, and sexually assaults each in turn. This is but one instance, repeated again and again, of him abusing his female children across the years. Finally, one exhausted victim tearfully describes her victimization to an English neighbor, who contacts the police. The father is questioned, confesses, and is arrested, spending several years in prison. Long before the civil authorities intervene, the father is sanctioned by the Amish church. He confesses his sins to the assembled membership. He is placed under a short Bann and excommunicated for six weeks. Shunned during this period of reflection and remorse, he returns to express repentance for his behavior and be restored to full fellowship. Following biblical teaching, his sins are forgiven and forgotten. "Forgiven" does not mean that his victims, including his wife as the mother of these traumatized children, are at peace with what occurred. It does mean that they are determined to resolve all that has happened and find a way to accept this man, despite the trauma he created in their lives. They, too, set a foot on the road to forgiveness, determined to walk that path to the end.

I have testified several times in Amish child sexual abuse cases. Each time, I remind the court and those assembled that we perceive a paradox. How can the Amish forgive those from the world who commit murder but also fail to punish their own people who abuse children? Instead of an inconsistency, it is better understood as opposite sides of the same coin. Forgiveness is ingrained in Amish beliefs. We stand in awe when they forgive a man, undoubtedly delusional, who callously murdered five little girls and traumatized unknown numbers of children and parents. And we pass the harshest judgment when they forgive a man who sexually abuses his own children. We see two entirely different scenarios. They see only Jesus's admonition: forgive.

The antithesis of these beliefs is so deeply ingrained for those of us in the mainstream culture that it is almost impossible to comprehend the Amish viewpoint. The heteronormative, for Americans and Canadians, precludes any acceptance of those who violate the vulnerability of children without (a) a period of incarceration, (b) a period of mental health treatment, (c) visible and ongoing shame and remorse, and (d) some form of monitoring to ensure public safety. The efficacy of these efforts is secondary to the need to create sufficiently harsh consequences. To forgive and forget such heinous behavior is to betray the sacred trust of childhood given to the adult caretakers of these innocent lives.

Lest this chapter skew the perception of the heteronormative in Amish culture, they place a strong value on the safety and well-being of children. They are familiar with Jesus's rebuke to his disciples, found in the gospel stories of both Matthew and Luke. As those followers attempted to protect their Savior from unnecessary intrusions on his time, they dismissed little ones who clamored to see him. When Jesus became aware of what they were doing, he said, "Suffer little children, and forbid them not, to come unto me: for such is the kingdom of heaven."[2] The Amish want to protect and preserve the innocence of childhood.

The safety of these vulnerable members of the culture is nevertheless balanced against the need to forgive, the noblest reason why child abuse goes unreported, as it so often has.[3] Among Amish clergy members I have known who grappled with the decision of whether to report abuse, their struggle was sincere. Is it a true forgiveness on their part if they report the penitent sinner to civil authorities? For those settlements that do not have liaisons or working systems of support integrated with governmental agencies, this is a pressing concern that preys on the conscience of their leadership.

There are pragmatic concerns in play, too. No legal violation runs a greater risk of interlocking their lives with the outside world than child abuse. The right of the state to protect its highest-risk citizens trumps civil rights of privacy, which are abrogated as state-appointed representatives investigate the allegations. This civil intrusion contributes to Amish reluctance about reporting child abuse or allowing reports of it to occur. One is reminded of Bill Clinton's famous "Don't ask, don't tell" compromise for gays in the military. The same attitude exists among the Amish about sharing reports of abuse, lest the worldly authority obtain a foothold in the community.

The other practical concern arises from the foundations of a hierarchical culture and was addressed briefly at the end of the preceding chapter. The Amish heteronormative places males over females, with clergy assuming the greatest authority, followed by mature adults. If the accusations of a child can topple that authority, the control invested in the patriarchy is at risk. Thus it becomes a self-serving function to minimize the impact of abuse allegations. This chapter examines the ramifications of the Amish penchant to sidestep direct confrontation with this traumatizing issue.

Sex Offenses in a Collective Culture

The trauma created by sexual abuse against children is well documented.[4] Research on treatment interventions with those who sexually offend highlights their diversity.[5] While it has been long hypothesized that there is no single, definitive reason why adults molest children, empirical studies increasingly support a multiple-pathways model as they uncover differing dynamics. Adolescents who offend act on the basis of the need for power and control, a delinquent predisposition, or an immature, regressed effort to meet their sexual needs.[6] Adults also act from a position of dominance, asserting power and control over a potential sexual partner. At least one form of pedophilia is coming into focus as a sexual age orientation.[7] For those drawn to prepubescent children, theirs may be a desire for romantic involvement. Ironically, when abuse arises from this orientation, it can include greater empathy toward the child. Membership in groups such as b4uact or similar support systems reflect the emotional and psychological distress those who are thus inclined encounter from their sexual object choice.[8]

Still, an understanding of the dynamics underlying pedophilic interests is nascent. The primary effort has been intervention for those apprehended, focused on cognitive and cognitive-behavioral treatments to elicit behavior change.[9] The understandings that have developed center on the actuarial risk for reoffending and, as such, use tangible, measurable criteria.[10] The complex interpersonal and intrapersonal dynamics of those who sexually offend thus far elude a commonly accepted theory.

Given these facts, the ability to explain the role of sexual offenses in Amish culture is tentative. Nonetheless, some observations are possible by extrapolation. The cultural control of sexual behavior differs. For the Amish, sex has a primary purpose, that of procreation. The fulfillment of sexual desire for other purposes risks being categorized as a sin when that desire is fulfilled in a manner, or with a sexual object, incapable of reproducing. This is true whether the object is same-sex, animal, or child. Shame and guilt therefore attend any such sexual acting out, because it is both hedonistic and unnatural. In mainstream culture, the primary taboo is forcing or coercing children into behaviors they are too young to comprehend or in which they cannot meaningfully participate. In Amish culture, the sinner violates not only the taboo of participating in sexual behavior with a partner too young to understand, but also that of engaging in a pleasure-based use of sex.

Amish who sexually offend presumably act from the same motives that drive those who do so in the mainstream culture.[11] Adolescent acting out, as well as adult needs for power and control, are a primary reason for engaging in sexual activity with a partner who is younger and unable to participate in an egalitarian manner.[12] Likewise, a certain number of Amish adults are presumed to exhibit a sexual age orientation that focuses their attraction primarily or exclusively on children. A significant cultural difference is the accessibility of potential victims in Amish settlements compared with the mainstream. With an average of seven children per family, the presence of a single potential perpetrator may place many more youth at risk than is true in non-Amish families, but the actual extent to which this increases the risk and frequency of abuse in their communities is not documented.

In a hierarchical culture, it is already commonplace for males to have a higher social status than women, and for older persons to hold greater social standing than younger ones. Older siblings commonly provide childcare and supervision for their younger brothers and sisters. These stepdown expectations are the model to which every Amish child is exposed. Therefore, if an older male—a clergy member, father, uncle, sibling, or cousin—invokes his authority, a younger child, particularly a female, is unlikely to resist. Nor, of greater importance, is she likely to report his behavior. She now feels hurt, confused, or angry, aware that the behavior transgressed a boundary, but finds herself entangled in the need to decide which boundary is paramount. On the one hand, she has been asked to engage in an inappropriate sexual or pseudosexual activity. On the other, reporting such behavior violates respect for an older male authority figure. She is more likely to internalize feelings of shame and guilt than resolve this dilemma in favor of her own rights, thereby risking the disapproval of family and friends and usurping the balance of power.

This experience parallels and amplifies what often occurs in mainstream culture. Children too young to fully comprehend what is being asked, or the behavior in which they are engaging, are manipulated into playing a game, sharing secrets, or being instructed not to tell others, often with threats of punishment or consequences. This use of force, ranging on a continuum from coercion to overt threats to the infliction of physical pain, elicits the cooperation of a younger, weaker individual with someone older and more powerful. In a patriarchal hierarchy, the expectation for cooperation is in place long before any sexual abuse is initiated. The need for grooming behaviors or manipulation to prepare the victim for actual sexual activity,[13] prominent in mainstream culture, is far less for the Amish, as is the need to elicit secrecy. The victim understands implicitly, without the need for force, that control over the interaction rests with the perpetrator.

In addition, among the Amish as well as the mainstream, victim *and* perpetrator may feel shame and guilt. This dilemma for the victim is not necessarily ameliorated upon discovery. Responsibility may be parsed for older victims (discussed in the following sections), and, as noted above, the guilt the perpetrator acknowledges may be that of violating the rights of a child, running the risk of discovery, and acting out sexually in a hedonistic manner, the latter a type of guilt more common for those with strong fundamental Christian values. At other times, as the perpetrator distorts the heteronormative hierarchy to meet his needs, a recognition of guilt is even less, as his response twists into an egocentric entitlement. The perpetrator then feels empowered by the act of abuse, leaving the victim to her guilt and shame. Again, this is relatively common in both mainstream and Amish cultures. It is the intensity of the affective experience, and the way victims and perpetrators are managed if the secret is exposed, that differs among the Amish.

The Church and Sex Offenses

The reaction to the revelation that one's child has been hurt is powerful and visceral. The initial response of parents, whether Amish or English, on discovering that their child has been sexually abused is shock. If the person offending and the victim are members of the same family,[14] the devastating truth is accompanied by rage, denial, or a combination of both emotions, depending on the role and status of the perpetrator and efforts at self-protection. This may include erratic problem solving, based on irrational logic but designed to return the family system to its status quo. These efforts are not only ineffective, but fail to provide relief to the victim or meaningful intervention for the person who committed the abuse. Despite the vituperative anger parents feel, the thought of the consequences to be meted out to a loved one who was the perpetrator can be frightening.

Regardless, a family's response is predicated on its history, and even in a collective culture, family histories are unique. If that history includes pervasive, systemic intimidation and fear, revelation of the abuse can be received with apparent apathy toward the perpetrator. This is particularly true for a father, grandfather, uncle, or other male figure in an authoritarian role. A patriarchy amplifies that authority, as well as the corresponding likelihood of a passive response. The frightened reaction of long-term victims can then become a hostility projected toward those who attempt to intervene. Victimization thus expands far beyond the member targeted for abuse and encompasses all of those in the family system who find themselves helpless in the face of unfolding events. Even for Amish families who choose to address abuse, the expectations of the culture create a different trajectory than that anticipated when civil authorities intervene with non-Amish families.

A glaring difference is the following repeated observation, made here and elsewhere in academic works on the Amish: the arbitration of sin falls under the authority of the church. Donald Kraybill refers to confession as "Amish therapy."[15] The matrix of confession includes two types: voluntary and requested. Voluntary confessions are initiated by individuals, based on personal conscience. They acknowledge a transgression to the ministers, who choose whether it should be made public. Requested confessions are mandated by the clergy. They address an observed or reported behavior that violates the Ordnung or otherwise offends expectations. (If the person offending is not baptized there is no formal confession, but, instead, an informal expectation of a penitent demeanor.) The act of confession, in the ideal, has a specific model. The penitent church member confesses a sin to the minister, or does so in the presence of assembled Christian brothers and sisters. The act is cathartic, or cleansing. Once the sinner purges himself of the sin and receives forgiveness (after submitting to a consequence, if the transgression requires it), genuine repentance means a full restoration into fellowship. The sin is forgiven and forgotten, a stain removed without a trace, because of Jesus's atonement.

Too often, however, reality intrudes. While the act of confession can be cleansing, many also find it humiliating. Moreover, the concept of forgetting a sin is noble, but egregious sins are catalogued and retained in social memory. This is logical in a high-context culture, where the assumption that a behavior can be forgotten is paradoxical to the need to collect information. As a result, those who commit sexual offenses remain known in their family, their church, their settlement, and beyond. They have been returned to full fellowship, so no overt prejudice is tolerated, but the awareness of their proclivity remains.

Unfortunately, repentance and atonement resolve some sins more effectively than others. Behaviors symptomatic of addictions, compulsions, or an ingrained pattern recur, despite the best intents of penitent and church. Therefore, it is not unusual to find a member offering repeated confessions of sexual abuse, either in the same church or in different churches or settlements, as those who offend struggle to contain their acting out. Each time, the process of contrition begins anew. The penitent confesses; punishment is meted out, if necessary; the penitent is restored to fellowship; and the sin is forgiven and forgotten, its memory left to dissipate over time.

Some among the clergy insist that the offending member attend an Amish residential treatment facility. And some settlements demonstrate a far-sighted and noble effort to work with local authorities to ensure that both the offending member and his victims receive needed help.[16] These are cutting-edge efforts to address an ongoing mental health issue. Still, the spectrum of responses is weighted toward the traditional cycle of church discipline.

The perception that the Amish shield those who commit sex offenses from the consequences of their actions is disturbing in itself. Yet there is still another layer to the challenge of child sexual abuse in this collective culture. At times, conservative Amish churches parse responsibility for sexual abuse between the perpetrator and the victim. The degree of responsibility accorded the victim is based on numerous factors, including age, maturity, and the level of consensual participation. As the victim is not normally baptized into the church, she is not required to make a formal confession. Still, she is expected to own up to her part of the abuse and respond accordingly. While this is neither a consistent perception nor one condoned by all Amish, the attitude exists among churches in many affiliations and settlements.

In the twenty-first century, the concept of victim responsibility is appalling to the mainstream. For a culture that retains a patriarchal system reminiscent of the United States in the early to mid-twentieth century, this view is less shocking.[17] It can be perceived as necessary to maintain the equilibrium of cultural (dis)parity, the emphasis on humility for all members of the sect, and the attitude of forgiveness anticipated as a core value. The church assumes the role of a loving but firm parent, meting out discipline to ensure the ultimate well-being of its children. That well-being translates to an eternity with God, a goal that cannot be attained if the insidious potential for sin is not rooted out wherever it is found. No matter how minute the sliver of responsibility a victim has, it is better that she acknowledges her part, rather than run the risk of an eternal separation from her heavenly home.

This spiritual concern, both for victim responsibility and for the church as the primary disciplinarian in matters of child abuse, again falls within a spectrum. All Amish emphasize the temporal and transient nature of one's time on earth, with an eternal life to follow. They all hope for an eternity in the presence of God. Still, differences exist, not only among conservative and progressive groups, but also within these groups, as to the need to advocate for victims. These differences are predicated on the importance of alleviating suffering in this life and the extent to which suffering imitates the pain of Jesus, to be shouldered without complaint, just as he did. The response to child abuse does not remain a pure spiritual motivation. It is here once again that spiritual concerns and practical expectations of power and control merge to influence the heteronormative.

The Amish Politics of Child Sexual Abuse

"Politics" can be an emotionally charged word, implying artful and, at times, dishonest practices. It is not used here as a derogatory term, but in its meaning as the art or science of government. The Amish church is charged with political oversight of the culture, a position of power and control. In that role, it monitors and controls the behavior of those who sexually offend against children. The intrusion of social service or law enforcement agencies supplants the church and threatens its status within the social order. Civil justice bangs on the door, demanding interviews, investigations, and external policies. It runs roughshod over the decision-making power imbued by the Amish heteronormative order. No external authority, program, or issue is more frightening to them than agencies that protect children. This is state control at its most intrusive, the prerogative of the government to advocate for its most helpless citizens by superseding spiritual, religious, and cultural values in order to supervise and, if necessary, remove children from their homes.

In one example, an Amish bishop in Indiana wrote to a social service agency caseworker who removed children from an abusive family. The bishop agreed with the caseworker's assessment that the children were in danger in the home. But he also stated in his letter, "Having children placed in a foster home for 24 to 72 hours causes an additional trauma. Even if it would be an Amish foster home the parents would probably be complete strangers to the children."[18] In a dialogue with me after the fact, he clarified that there was no compelling reason, ever, to remove children from their home. For him, the controls that could be implemented in a collective, high-context culture mitigated the risk to the children's safety and were less damaging to their emotional well-being.

At a practical level, the Amish, similar to other minorities in America, do not perceive social services or law enforcement as efficacious.[19] The prevailing assumption that interventions offer assistance and improve situations is viewed askance by groups who see themselves as misunderstood, ineptly served, or ballyhooed, with little or no follow-through. In the case of the Amish, an effort to create liaisons between agencies and settlements is often effective. Yet in a high-context, collective culture, relationships are established with individuals, not with agencies. Accordingly, as these bureaucracies experience staff turnover and policy changes, bridge programs collapse or must be repeatedly renewed.

Agencies themselves, once involved, also face difficult choices. Charging or prosecuting a member of the Amish church for an offense can send a clear message that certain behaviors will not be tolerated. (The Amish themselves rarely press charges. The use of legal force is taboo for a nonresistant people.) It can also dampen the reporting of similar behaviors by the Amish from that settlement for many years to come. One possible response becomes lighter or nonexistent sentences for Amish who sexually offend, recognizing the need to respond to a collective culture in a different manner, in order to encourage ongoing reporting. The alternative is an effort to establish equal treatment of all citizens under the law, knowing that reporting by the Amish will almost certainly be suppressed.

The potential for foster care, mentioned above, is also problematic. Placing an Amish child in an English foster home protects the victim, but it also exposes the child to a novel environment. The culture shock of a home with television and video games—not to mention interactions with other foster children who are also there, due to severe disruptions in their non-Amish homes—creates a risk for exposure to a world for which the child is unprepared. A subsequent return to the family of origin creates a modern-day Marco Polo, sharing explorations of a mysterious world with that Amish child's incredulous siblings. The alternative, to foster a child in an Amish home, is either to make a placement with a relative and hope the family abides by agency rules for supervision, or hope for availability in one of the few licensed Amish foster homes.

Bishops vary in their insight and psychological sophistication. Some have a deep empathy with and understanding of the potential for trauma due to sexual abuse. They perceive the unremitting nature of sexual urges that those who offend, particularly adults, all too frequently experience. A select few may initiate an interaction with civil authorities. This would be a conscious decision to renege on the authority of the Amish church and defy the heteronormative control of their culture over sexual behavior. It is neither a decision made lightly nor frequently. A bishop willing to engage with civil authority will often do so only in the most heinous or intractable cases. The collective society therefore has a vested interest in maintaining power through their social order when sexual abuse of children comes to light. It does so by controlling the flow of information about the abuse, positioning the church as the arbiter to mediate justice, and (for some) parsing blame between perpetrator and victim.

The prevalent view held by those responsible for the well-being of children in our society says that dividing the blame is a blatant means of maligning females. Since the preponderance of victims are female children, the patriarchy shifts responsibility for the actions of male perpetrators whenever possible, scapegoating and disenfranchising helpless girls. In reality, these children bear no responsibility for having been forced into behaviors that were neither sought nor desired, and to hold them accountable is a miscarriage of justice and a misrepresentation of developmental capability that is sexist and cruel.

With no dispute about the merits of that argument, another perspective is grounded in the principles originally espoused by Franz Boas's cultural relativism.[20] In this view, whether it is apropos to blame the victim is not the decision of an outside agent. Amish culture regulates its sexual mores through its own processes, and it remains for those of us in the mainstream to respect the fact that it occurs. We need not accept their heteronormative as our own, but our indignant remonstrations do nothing to change the attitude of their culture or the expectations it holds toward its perpetrators and victims.

An example clarifies this point. I was working with a young Amish man who severely sexually abused his sister while she was in early adolescence. The case had been reported to the state authorities, hence my involvement. In rapid succession, three therapists assigned to work with the victim were unable to establish rapport, much less make progress, and I was asked to intervene. They were indeed a difficult family, some of the most conservative Old Order Amish (in use of technology and distance from the world) that I had counseled.[21] I agreed to act as a liaison to find support for the victim, although I would not see her myself. (I counsel both victims and those who offend, but not victims and the person who perpetrated the abuse against them.) After casting about, it seemed as though she had a good relationship with a previous teacher from her Amish school, who was willing to act as a mentor. I met with the teacher and discussed the situation.

In doing so, this teacher asked me a general question about an English counselor's perceptions of responsibility and the victim. I was terse. The girl's older brother initiated and coerced the abuse and was fully responsible. This Amish teacher with an eighth grade education, squaring off with a doctoral-level psychologist, handled me well. She began by agreeing with everything I had said. She then noted the rejection the victim would experience in her family, church, and community if she did not assume at least partial responsibility. I reluctantly concurred with a plan to allow the victim limited owner-ship in the abuse. She would ask forgiveness for her part. Over time, it became obvious that the teacher understood the situation far better than I. It was not a belief I could accept, but it was a belief I needed to respect. The controls in place in the Amish church in which I was working were inviolable, at least to English professionals.

Lest the Amish be scapegoated for their failure to appreciate the needs of the child, we in the mainstream culture blind ourselves to the difficulties we create in attempting to advocate for and protect our children. As a psychologist in private practice, I provide services outside Amish communities: to social service agencies, courts, pros-ecutors, and criminal attorneys. Over the years, I have assessed and testified both for and against persons who have sexually offended against children. The likelihood of charges being filed in a case, those charges actually being pressed, a plea bargain being offered versus a trial, and the harshness of the sentence depend, in large part, on the monetary means of the defendant and the socioeconomic status of the victim. All too often, financial resources and social niceties trump the severity of the crime in deciding treatment and punishment.[22]

The Amish heteronormative view is complex, intertwined with both spiritual and practical demands that drive the mechanics of a response to sexual abuse. The spiritual demand returns to a core view that this earthly sojourn is temporary. The hope is for salvation, an eternal life with God. Confession and forgiveness occur in the church. State-controlled mechanisms to exact consequences lack this ultimate power. Both those who offend and those who have been victims of the offense, particularly if they are old enough to understand what occurred, may be expected to ask forgiveness. It is far better for the latter to suffer temporary shame in admitting their part in sexual abuse than to risk permanent separation from God.

From a practical standpoint, the patriarchy is assaulted by the threat of an external authority. The clergy act as God's emissaries on earth. To allow social service personnel or law enforcement agents free rein in the community risks the ministry's control. Such worldly emissaries both usurp the power of the clergy and align with female children. The well-being of the hierarchy cannot be dismissed so easily. It is not the act of abuse, or even those who abuse per se, that the Amish hierarchy wishes to protect. It is the risk of prying open a door shut firmly against heteronormative values that could disable the patriarchy and poison the spiritual values central to the culture. With their eyes fixed firmly on that doorway, leaders too often fail to cast even a glance behind at the suffering their actions ignore.

Proactive and Reactive Responses to Sexual Offending

Compared with efforts in the mainstream culture, sexual abuse is minimally addressed by the Amish. Instead, they make proactive efforts to respond to sinful actions before they can arise. These efforts, however, are in keeping with the circumspect manner in which all sexual issues are confronted. Two widely circulated brochures developed by Amish writers discuss sexual abuse. They couch their language carefully. Both *A Fence or an Ambulance?* and *Walk in the Light* speak to sexual sin and the need to confine sex to a marital relationship.[23] They also address issues such as zoophilia and child sexual abuse. On the other hand, they use the term "private parts" and remain vague in their description of behaviors that are taboo. It is left to the reader to understand that this range of sexual and sexualized acts, from flirtations to overtly inappropriate behaviors to violating the rights of others, vary in severity. These brochures also highlight the ambiguity with which these issues are addressed in the community and filter down to discussions with children.

For example, *Walk in the Light* includes a section that reads in part as follows:

What actually are sexual sins? If done to a minor, these are also child abuse.

A. It is indecent exposure.
B. It is touching others' private parts, or having them touch ours, whether on bare skin or on top of clothes.
C. It is uncovering yourself or others, or asking them to uncover themselves for your pleasure.
D. It is suggestive sexual conversation—conversation that either gratifies self or arouses others.
E. It is bestiality, which is the use of animals for sexual gratification.

All sexual acts outside of marriage are sin.

This unqualified listing of sexual sins reinforces the heteronormative expectation of sex primarily for procreation. Mainstream culture categorizes sexual misconduct by the degree and severity of the violation. In part, this Amish lack of scaling reflects the anticipation that life on earth entails hardship, while the hoped-for heavenly reward is an eternity of bliss. We are given to suffer and forgive. Therefore, to focus too long or too intensely on sins committed against us runs the risk of failing to forgive and falling into the sin of judgment ourselves. Despite this preference, there are other booklets addressing sexual behavior, ones more sweeping in their scope and specific in their approach, offered by Amish publishers.[24]

Such an effort to forgive is meritorious. What it lacks is an embedded system to address behaviors that are symptomatic of pervasive clinical syndromes or enduring character traits. In the case of child sexual abuse, the need for governance and control of both those who offend and their victims fails to consider the repetitive nature of these behaviors and the traumatic emotional injuries they produce. Too frequently, child sexual abuse becomes a fire bell in the night, but not as a way to alert the patriarchy that a victim is in distress. It clangs a warning that external authorities may intervene if they do not manage the problem internally.

The Amish do not condone, nor do they tolerate, child sexual abuse. They do believe in an internal system of intervention and control to manage those who offend. Likewise, those who perpetrate abuse and their victims respond with an awareness that the former often has impunity within Amish culture, efforts to change that status notwithstanding.[25] An interweaving of heteronormative, patriarchal protection and spiritual beliefs combine to create a strong resistance to change in the attitude that instances of child sexual abuse, as with other sins, are best handled by ecclesiastical as opposed to civil control. The protection of Amish children from sexual abuse remains one of the most difficult areas of intervention.

Chapter Eight

Victorian's Secret

Paraphilias and the Amish

The following excerpt is taken from a story published in a booklet created for Plain people struggling with sexual sin.[1]

At age thirteen I discovered a world of self-applied ecstasy—and was immediately addicted. . . . This was a "high" I hadn't experienced before. Those first four years I wasn't completely sure if it was right or not. Then at seventeen, someone made a confession at church for *selbst beflectung.* I asked mother what that meant after we got home and was shocked to know that I had actually been sinning all this time. Fantasies always led to my acting out in masturbation. In real life I was shy and bashful with women. In acting out I made advances and charmed them into having sex. I loathed myself. I hated myself. "I will never do this again," I often decided. I often thought of how to quit, and wondered how to do it. I finally decided on castration, though I couldn't bring myself to go through the pain.

I knew my problem would quit after I married . . . but what a surprise. Finally, I was ordained a minister, and for a month I could feel—literally in the air—the prayers of the church to help me. The presence of the Holy Ghost was in the air. During this time I was not tempted, and by practicing a daily relationship with Jesus I have remained clean for five years now. Still, every day one has to recommit to be clean; has to recommit to love his wife no matter what; has to recommit to have a daily relationship to adore and revere the Lord.

Paraphilias, or fetishes, as this vignette demonstrates, are culturally defined. While this man may be depicting a compulsive behavior, it is equally possible that he describes his heteronormative distress with what other cultures perceive as a normal sexual outlet. This chapter analyzes the Amish prohibition on sexual behaviors that do not lead to procreation and the way in which this injunction is handled.[2]

Queen Victoria allegedly quipped, "I feel sure that no girl would go to the altar if she knew all." Victoria's vaunted efforts to preserve the sanctity of British morality are now the stuff of legend. In contrast, postmodern culture is suffused by a combination of relaxed mores and sexually explicit material within hailing distance of any Wi-Fi connection. It is tempting to twist another of her (reputed) dour one-liners and say, "We *are* amused." For the Amish, however, the firm expectation continues that sex and sexuality has a niche—albeit a utilitarian, God-given role, as essential as breathing. Perhaps not to the overwrought extreme that the naïve quote above suggests but, nevertheless, a carefully crafted, purified incarnation of the meaning and purpose of sex in their lives.

If sex serves the noble primary purpose of procreation, there is no room for paraphilias. Psychiatry defines these quirks as ". . . any intense and persistent sexual interest, other than sexual interest in genital stimulation or preparatory fondling with phenotypically normal, physically mature, consenting human partners."[3] Paraphilic attraction can attach to any tangible object (e.g., a body part, a living organism) or behavior (e.g., observing or being observed in various stages of undress). For example, the (in)famous foot fetish attaches sexual arousal to feet. The mechanism by which this occurs is easily understood via classical conditioning.[4] The experience of a positive stimulus (presumably orgasm, or, at a minimum, strong sexual arousal) occurs in close temporal proximity to contact with or observation of feet. The positive stimulus therefore becomes associated with the object. Particularly if this occurs multiple times, feet become a source of arousal. If the positive stimulus is sufficiently intense, it takes relatively few trials for the association to become embedded as a sexual object choice.

Classical conditioning plays out in the same way with other paraphilias. A positive stimulus (orgasm or strong sexual arousal) occurs in close temporal proximity subsequent to either cognitions (fantasies) of a specific act or the behavior itself. Through cognitive rehearsal (repeated fantasizing) or actually engaging in the act, the positive stimulus and the behavior are associated, and the behavior becomes a source of arousal. Nonetheless, there are limits to the validity of paraphilic theory based on classical conditioning. For example, complex paraphilias require a more elegant model. As mentioned in the previous chapter, at least some forms of pedophilia are conceptualized as a sexual age orientation, inclusive of complex interpersonal dynamics not presumed to be present in a simple fetish.

Mainstream culture parses the morality of engaging in paraphilic behaviors. Those that involve non-consenting individuals, or individuals who cannot give knowledgeable consent, are morally negative. Therefore, exposing oneself to unsuspecting passersby (exhibitionism), attempting to view nude or semi-nude individuals without their consent or knowledge (voyeurism), or making obscene phone calls to an unsuspecting and unwilling participant (telephone scatologia) are all considered to be offensive, as well as illegal in almost all locales. Those that do not create victims are more often perceived as morally neutral (e.g., cross-dressing or sexual role play), although they may engender a personal revulsion or raise questions about self-esteem for those who do not share the fetish. For example, the experiences of play with urine (urophilia), physical dominance and submission (bondage and discipline), or even re-creation of the experience of infancy via diapers (adult diaper enthusiasts) are usually solitary or involve consenting participants. Although these activities may still be considered troubling by some, they are less likely to draw moral fire. Normally, a fetish becomes a moral wrong with the involuntary participation of a second party in the activity. Sexual deviancy in object choice has a long history of moral and legal ambiguity,[5] diagnostic confusion,[6] and cultural relativism.[7]

A moral curve for differing paraphilias is a logical evolution of sexuality in mainstream culture. Within its heteronormative, sex no longer serves the primary purpose of procreation. It is a means of experiencing pleasure and engaging with others. In other words, sexuality serves as an identity. The logical outcome is freedom to explore and experiment within the context of behaviors that were once considered deviant sexual encounters.

And for the Amish? Paraphilias have no place in their heteronormative design. Beyond that view, however, their cultural definition of a paraphilia is far more expansive than ours. It could be modified to read "any intense and persistent sexual interest, other than sexual interest in genital stimulation or preparatory fondling with phenotypically normal, physically mature, consenting human partners *of the opposite gender by birth, when married, that ultimately leads to procreation.*"

This chapter examines the nature and role of paraphilias among the Amish. These are an insidious threat to heteronormative boundaries, since their genesis arises within the culture and is not an external morality to be challenged. They are suppressed whenever possible, and, when revealed, are an embarrassment to be addressed as quickly as possible.

Paraphilias in Amish Culture

Psychiatry's concise definition notwithstanding, paraphilia has no universal characterization accepted by the mental health community.[8] The transition from the fourth to the fifth edition of the *Diagnostic and Statistical Manual of Mental Disorders* of the American Psychiatric Association emphasizes the discomfiting nature of the sexual object choice or behavior, not the sexual object choice or behavior itself.[9] Ironically, this subjective view, emphasizing emotional distress, lends credence to a variety of behaviors being considered as disorders, based on cultural norms.

In addition, then, to indiscrete object choices and behaviors that make the list in mainstream culture, the Amish include masturbation, oral and anal sex, and manual stimulation of a partner. Each is a taboo activity for at least some churches, utilized for purposes of pleasure distinct from procreation. As the list grows, it becomes evident that every Amish individual, over time and on a repeated basis, must engage in paraphilic activities that violate their Ordnung.

Years ago, I occasionally co-led psychoeducational groups of Amish adolescent males who were referred following their arrests on alcohol-related charges.[10] One group in particular was uniquely bright and creative. In their unusually broad-minded zeitgeist, they enjoyed role plays. One evening they challenged their Amish co-leader and me to role play a confession in church. We agreed, provided they could tie the purpose back to the class. As bright and oppositional adolescents, they could. We asked for a sin to be confessed. "A guy had sex with a cow," said one of the bolder youth. "Come on," I interjected, "Use something someone would really confess." At that moment a hush fell over the room. The brash youngster who had spoken with such confidence now looked uncertain, started to speak again, and fell silent. Our Amish co-leader finally broke the tense quiet. "He's serious," the co-leader said, followed by looks of profound relief on the boys' faces. I can state with certainty that not only was it the only therapy session in which I have role played, much less processed the outcome of zoophilia, but it is also the only session in which such a role play could conceivably have had the positive effect it did.

There are several pertinent facets to this vignette, confirmed in my hastily assembled post-session dialogue with the Amish co-leader.[11] First, although there was a healthy dose of adolescent titillation in the introduction of this confession, zoophilia was sufficiently common that none of the boys considered it too extreme to mention. Second, confession is limited to the presence of church members and, in this settlement, was expected to remain confidential. This meant that the sanctity of the confession was routinely violated, since these boys were still in Rumspringa and well aware of what occurred. Third, their nonjudgmental attitude about the act itself suggested that this paraphilia was a relatively common sexual outlet.

The lesson learned was that paraphilias may be limited in terms of open discussion, but they are commonly known in Amish settlements, evidence again of the repressive hypothesis. Whether these young men would have been as forthright and honest had they been baptized and faced the risk of confession themselves is an open question. It is an arresting example of youth modeling adult behaviors that they have not yet fully internalized. Such modeling is the way in which they prepare themselves for adult roles. In this case, it is instructive to consider whether their play prepared them not only for the mechanics of confession, but also for the accountability they would face there.

Personal Deviance in a Collective Culture

In a collective, high-context culture, individual identity still exists. The purpose is not to create interchangeable automatons, incapable of independent thought. But, once formed, too much autonomy for that individual identity is not encouraged. The goal in finding oneself is not the pursuit of personal ambition. One learns instead to merge personal identity into the will of the greater whole. Ironically, like the military they reject on the grounds of nonresistance, the Amish instill a belief in the individual as an element of a larger unit, not a freestanding component.

That collective standard plays out in most expressions of daily living, including the attainment of material possessions. The Ordnung specifies limitations on technology.[12] Everything, from the type of lighting in the house (from battery or solar power in progressive Amish homes to kerosene lanterns in conservative Amish dwellings) to specific standards for types of dress, is codified here. The reasonably observant outsider can discern the settlement from which a person hails by their buggy (e.g., open or closed, color, accordion vs. sliding panel doors, and rear windows), or the style of clothing (e.g., aprons, pleats, and colors in women's dresses; coverings; colors in men's shirts;

buttons or pins for fastening; and style of men's hats). The system controls its members by regulating accoutrements and actions.

Those who deviate significantly from these expectations can expect to be reprimanded and called to return to appropriate behaviors. If they fail to do so, more severe consequences follow, but rarely is this necessary. The mere disapproval of peers is a sufficient force to mediate change in the direction of social norms. Expressions of personal taste, for example, are not discouraged within the boundaries tolerated by the culture. Once personal taste crowds against these rules, however, the display must desist.

Personal identity, then, is firmly bounded by cultural identity. It is expected not only to yield to the heteronormative, but also to do so with grace and without complaint. The control exerted by the collective binds the sense of self. There is still freedom to pursue a variety of careers, to marry by choice, and to voice dissatisfaction with governance. Nevertheless, by joining the Amish church, one accepts its overt and covert power over virtually all aspects of one's life.

While the church can elucidate clear, implacable heteronormative boundaries, that does not change the risk for an individual to develop one or more paraphilias. Each person travels a road of emerging sexual identity, interests, and desires that is unique in its personal and social expression. Divergent sexual practices, including immoral and taboo sexual urges and behaviors, are a reality developed outside the awareness of the culture, but they are still subject to sanction by the church if they become known. The relativism the mainstream brings to such behaviors is intolerable among the Amish. Likewise, there are fewer gradations. A deviation from the primary purpose of procreation, regardless of its impact, can readily become a violation of the will of God.

For example, mainstream culture increasingly addresses the sexual needs of couples, without consideration of procreative capability. Erectile dysfunction, dyspareunia, and vaginismus receive medical services, mental health interventions, or a combination of both. In at least some cases, the interventions suggested involve foreplay or an accommodation to vaginal intercourse that, for the Amish, is paraphilic and therefore a questionable behavior.

Mental health professionals can find themselves conflicted about how best to meet the needs of their Amish clients with paraphilic dilemmas. For example, cross-dressing has become more and more innocuous as transgender identity is increasingly accepted. The power of social sanctions in mainstream society to create shame and to define fluid gender roles as a form of acting out has decreased dramatically. The majority of those in the mental health field focus on acceptance when providing services for genderfluid or transgender individuals, as well as those who remain further up the continuum and experience only the desire to cross-dress. Their purpose is often to minimize internalized discomfort with these psychological states and empower the client to recognize, explore, and pursue comfortable options—that is, acceptable expressions of a healthy sexuality. Only the most conservative counselors address them as compulsions that lie outside the realm of an individual's control.

In contrast, if a mental health professional sees an Amish person with an urge to cross-dress, that counselor is responding to a client coming from a collective culture. His or her identity is subsumed, yielding to the identity of the larger group. In this context, the urge becomes an unacceptable paraphilia and cannot be fulfilled without shame and guilt. Personal desire and a sense of self are in conflict with collective desire and a sense of community. If the client has come for help, that person is asking to be made whole by reducing the intensity of this personal demon. It is doubtful that such a client will recognize, much less voice, a transgender desire underlying these gender-rejecting behaviors, even if it is present. The surrounding culture is exerting power and control, defining this outlet as immoral.

The same principle applies to all paraphilias. Thus anything from quirophilia (partialism, or a hand fetish) to klismaphilia (the rare but anecdotally reported use of enemas for sexual gratification)[13] would, for a client from the mainstream culture, be a behavior for exploration and potential empowerment. At worst, if a paraphilia was accompanied by personal physical risk, any treatment would include harm-reduction education. These same behaviors would be considered deviant and disruptive for an Amish client and require a cessation approach.

The distress caused by paraphilias will vary. Individuals experiencing these behaviors juggle an intense personal shame at their acting out, as did the young adult whose story begins this chapter, with the desperate need to overcome their carnal desires and live in good standing with their cultural expectations.[14] When shame becomes overwhelming, confession is an option, but many Amish rapidly learn the lesson of the emotional tide that accompanies paraphilic acting out. Shame ebbs and flows in its intensity, and if one waits for the ebb tide, painful emotions are manageable. They therefore choose to avoid the public humiliation of confession and its accompanying expectation to modify sinful behavior. Presumably, too, at least some persons find relief and release for their paraphilias in the privacy of marriage. Heteronormative control can therefore be limited when the behaviors manifesting a paraphilia or an unacceptable identity can be hidden from public view.

Victims and Deviance in a Collective Culture

In any culture, whether paraphilias are considered an urge or compulsion, some create victims (beyond the child sexual abuse discussed in the preceding chapter). Mainstream culture relies on law enforcement and the judiciary to effectively manage such acting out. Amish reluctance to involve the government in their affairs has previously been discussed, and management of the sexual sin of paraphilias follows the same injunctions as any other. Accordingly, such behaviors are handled internally. The hierarchy of the social system and the power and control of the collective society manage miscreants, instead of pursuing legal indictment. Two examples demonstrate the informal and formal management of paraphilias.

In the first, a young married man was well liked and well respected in his community. He and his wife both came from good families in the settlement. They had one child and were expecting a second. He worked hard and was a good provider. His bishop was elderly and in poor health and would probably step down in the next few years. While campaigning was unthinkable, the young man was a logical nominee for the open position of minister that would occur when a new bishop was created. Then came the first whiff of scandal. He had been seen near a neighbor's home after dark. His presence there was uncertain, but a female had been in the shower and the question arose, Was this an attempt to spy on her? Several weeks later he was questioned by the deacon in his church and denied wrongdoing. Indeed, he was unsure, that long after the fact, if he was the person at the time and place named. No more was said, but the issue was never formally resolved.

In a collective society, word spreads quickly, and the story soon became common knowledge. As often happens, uncertainty about his identity as the person in question dropped away, as did uncertainty about whether the event even happened. It was now widely known that he was standing at the window while a neighbor undressed, but he denied the charge. Because it was the word of an upstanding male against that of a female, it was not pursued.

Without further evidence, a single incident might eventually recede, a temporary stain on his honor bleached away in the recesses of time. Then a second, and yet a third woman came forward to say that they had seen him lurking outside their windows while they dressed. These allegations could have been true, but they also could have been conjured by the fear of a potential "peeper" (the term used) in the neighborhood. There was no way to be certain, for the women were describing a shadowy figure and expressing their suspicion that it was the young man in question. He was visited by the deacon once again, a longer visit this time. Because he continued to vehemently deny the behavior and no credible witness would state that she had seen him, no confession was ever sought.

Despite the weakness of the evidence and the lack of a confession, three incidents were more than the community could tolerate. He was, in the opinion of most, a voyeur.[15] His steadfast denial and refusal to confess did not absolve him. The majority believed the allegations, and his sins were neither forgiven nor forgotten. No overt confrontation occurred, but from time to time, shared conversations in the community kept his name and supposed transgressions alive. For several years this remained the case. The most obvious fallout occurred when, as predicted, his bishop retired and a new minister was chosen by lot for his church. The suspected man did not receive sufficient nominations to be in the group.

Time, as they say, heals all wounds, and while his history as a peeper is still recalled, it is sufficiently distant that few, if any, hold it against him. He has moved on, as has the settlement. The power and control of a collective society in its expectations were clear, however. One of two possible scenarios was played out. Either this man met that control with personal integrity, refusing to submit to a charge for a sin he did not commit. Or his personal shame overrode his communal integrity, and he could not bring himself to confess to the assembled church, his neighbors, that he had violated the privacy of females in the area for purposes of sexual gratification. In either case, the weight of a collective conscience fell upon him, and he was reminded that he had been informally judged and found guilty.

In the second example, an Amish minister was accused of inappropriate conversation with a female neighbor. He would drop sexual statements (a form of coprolalia) in casual interactions and wait for her response. She tolerated this several times but eventually told her husband, who complained to the minister's bishop. (While the minister and the discomfited wife were neighbors, they lived in adjoining church districts.) The minister, duly chastened, gave a kneeling confession in church. He was then placed under a short Bann, resulting in his excommunication for six weeks. Per protocol, he was restored to full fellowship with the understanding that he was penitent and remorseful for the sins he had committed. He also met with the neighbor and her husband, acknowledged his behavior, apologized, and asked their forgiveness directly. He has since stated that while the relationship is not warm between the two households, it is cordial.

This minister's story was also well known in the settlement where he lived. Because he confessed his sin, was punished, and requested forgiveness from his victim, the same degree of rancor was not leveled toward him as was true for the previous transgressor. The influence of the collective society was able to be exerted through appropriate channels, and an indirect or subtle means of controlling his behavior was unnecessary. What makes the second story ironic is that virtually the same scenario had played out twenty years earlier, shortly after the man had married. He had engaged in similar coprolalia with a woman other than his wife and been confronted by the ministers. Because he had confessed and been punished then, as well, and because of the lapse of time between the two incidents, no further censure accrued the second time.[16]

Both examples indicate an awareness by the Amish that paraphilias exist and must be addressed. Consequences for such behavior will be applied. Provided that there is an attitude of repentance, forgiveness is bestowed, and the paraphilic action is formally forgotten, although it remains in the collective awareness. If such behaviors come to light, even if the evidence is inconclusive, the penitent is expected to assume responsibility. For those who fail to do so, a shadow falls across their status in the community, an informal disapproval that dissipate slowly over time.

These stories also highlight the importance of the formal hetero-normative. Submission to the will of the church, whether a demand or a more subtle pressure, is anticipated. Failure to submit, in the first instance, did not result in excommunication, or even Unfriddah. It did, however, elicit a display of disapproval, in essence a vote of no confidence by neighbors and church members, several years after the fact. In the second example, willingness to submit resulted in forgiveness and full restitution into fellowship.

Paraphilias in Marriage

As previously discussed, the serpent of paraphilias has no better place to hide in a collective culture than in the garden of marriage. This illicit knowledge primarily speaks to consensual paraphilias, fetishes in which a partner may wish to engage. A marital relationship holds the potential for a broad set of paraphilic interests. As a patriarchy, Amish men are the ultimate authority, but women hold significant influence in the bedroom. Sex serves the ultimate purpose of procreation, but the pleasure that accompanies the act, from foreplay to orgasm, is undeniable. Women are more likely to forego their own enjoyment in anticipation of serving men. They understand the benefits of making the act as arousing as possible for the male partner. With this power in mind, embellishments on staid and perfunctory sexual behavior take place. This can include, among others, sex toys, bondage and discipline, the use of pornographic materials, and non-procreative sexual positions. In the era prior to cell phones, I counseled an Amish couple who would take their buggy to a motel that offered adult movies available on demand, in order to watch pornography as a stimulus for their sexual encounters. They were seeking counseling for other issues. The paraphilia of pornography as a sexual enhancement was peripheral to the treatment they sought, and they were clear that they had neither the need nor the intention to stop this behavior.

Some or all of these activities are considered violations of various Ordnungs. While women may submit to their men's desires, the wholeheartedness of feminine engagement can vary, based on the extent to which they are accorded egalitarian involvement. All of which may sound strikingly familiar to non-Amish readers, at least at some stage of their lives.[17] It is ironic that one of the universal measures of control when it comes to leveling the playing field of a marital relationship is the give and take of sexual pleasure, but, on reflection, it is logical. The act occurs in private, the negotiations can be surreptitious, the ultimate outcome involves only the participants, and it does not (at least directly) influence their status in the broader community. For all of these reasons, sexual pleasure in the marriage bed, although it requires discretion, is one of the few areas in which an intrusive, collective, high-context culture is stopped. It is relegated to the hallway, forced to sit outside the bedroom door, curious but unenlightened.

There is a paradox that reinforces the heteronormative as couples find an outlet for paraphilic behaviors. On the one hand, their activity instills an identity separate from the collective culture. They are acting in ways that distance them from social norms and behaviors they are expected to uphold. There is now a tension, a secret, that binds them as they violate the rules. On the other hand, that same tension reminds them of heteronormative expectations. Whether titillating, anxiety-provoking, shameful, or a combination of these emotions, the creation of this identity, separate from an effort to meld into the collective, is a potent reminder of the endeavor to be a part of the larger culture. The fact that engaging in such behaviors must remain discrete reinforces the power of the larger group.

Managing Amish Paraphilic Behavior

How does the power and control exerted by the collective culture of the Amish impact paraphilic behaviors? Anecdotally, the vignettes above suggest that the heteronormative is at least as powerful as formal mechanisms of discipline. The minister accused of inappropriate comments to women appeared to constrain his behavior for twenty years after being made to confess it before relapsing into a similar transgression. The layperson accused of voyeurism, while never formally confessing, seemed to respond to less direct disapproval (i.e., visits from the deacon, failure to be nominated as a candidate for minister) by no longer engaging in these behaviors (if he ever had done so). And the support of his church for the minister whose vignette begins this chapter helped him resist the urge to masturbate.

In contrast, the need to keep dirty little secrets can strengthen the separation of an identity the culture works so hard to absorb, as the example of the Amish couple who used pornography as foreplay indicates. Every thought, emotion, action, and behavior that must be kept from others is one more building block in a wall that surrounds the private self. The dilemma becomes how to manage that self. If a private identity still reinforces the importance of the collective, then embracing the Amish church and its accompanying culture is a logical choice. But if that identity, including any paraphilic acting out, takes on an importance that outweighs the collective self, one's ability to accept the boundaries imposed by the culture becomes tenuous.

The fewer tenets of the Amish church a member can accept, and the less able that person is to live within its boundaries, the greater the shame and guilt, and the stronger the need to pay lip service only to its expectations. There are those who can achieve the latter superficial stance, but Amish parents work to instill a deep and abiding respect for Amish life that will last from cradle to grave. Only by embracing personal freedom can an individual raised in the Amish culture supersede these ties. That includes challenging the heteronormative and accepting sex as primarily pleasurable, without the guilt anticipated to accompany that mindset.

It is difficult to determine whether the Amish are more successful than the mainstream in suppressing non-consensual paraphilic interests. Theirs is a more disciplined culture.[18] This rigidity may therefore result in fewer displays of public acting out than we in the mainstream experience. The incidence of property and personal crimes perpetrated by Amish church members is certainly minuscule, compared with their English neighbors. It may be that the acting out of paraphilias in public is similarly constrained. Whether that constraint generalizes to private acting out is a consideration that cannot be determined.

At least one behavior that remains a paraphilia among the Amish has become a social movement in the mainstream. The next chapter examines responses to same-sex interests.

Chapter Nine

The Love That Won't Shut Up

Sexual Minorities and the Amish

How do the Amish view sexual minorities? The excerpt below is from a Pennsylvania man who long struggled with his same-sex feelings.[1]

Another Sunday. Oh, that I would not have to sit through another sermon like the one I heard today! As an adult, I can manage. It is the young boys and girls struggling to come to grips with their same-sex orientation who worry me. They find themselves alone, with nowhere to turn, and then listen to sermons teaching them they are bound for hell. That weighs on me so.

When I was just beginning to face my sexuality, preaching rarely touched on the subject of homosexuality. And even if it did, the evil example of Sodom and Gomorrah was used as a reminder, but that was all. It was a passing reference. Now, the media increasingly mentions homosexuality as an acceptable lifestyle, and more famous people "come out." Changes in the world that used to bypass us now stream into our community. At first, homosexuality in sermons was mentioned with the use of an archaic German word. The literal definition is "despoiler of little boys." It took me time to understand, but when I did? I was relieved. That was not a problem for me.

Then gay marriage hit the front page, and our church, joining a number of conservative and fundamental churches in the area, went ballistic. Mind you, our preachers didn't rant and rave. They didn't raise their voices and wave their arms. But they still managed to get their point across. At first it was subtle references. "What is going on in the world today," or "Legal but not biblical." Adults knew exactly what they meant. The topic continued as a top news story in the media, and as it did so, it became tolerable for the Amish to mention "gays."

As sermons included more accusations, I felt the first stirrings of real fear. Oh, I had long felt fear. Fear of eternal separation from God. Fear of discovery and what that would mean for my life as an Amish man. But those fears were constant companions. Because I knew not to discuss my sexuality openly, it seemed possible that I could continue to live in hiding. I might be miserable, but at least I was safe. No more. Gay marriage was a conversation everywhere. Amish sermons were blunt, and becoming even more condemning. Gays were thrilled by their hard-won victory. Me? I just wanted the whole subject to go away. Not because I objected to two people in love pledging a commitment. No, because I was frightened that its presence was shining a spotlight on same-sex issues in my community. I felt in danger. Freedom in the larger culture had placed me at risk.

The more the media covered the story, the more the preachers warned. I had come to accept myself for who and what I am. But I was listening to sermons that actually made me sick. And I did so sitting side by side on benches with fellow church members who were neighbors, friends, and relatives. And if they had known what I accepted about myself? They would turn on me, sickened and angry. I would lose everything. Literally everything. Except, of course, my integrity. You may read this and think, "Some would support you, regardless." They could not. If anyone failed to shun me, they would lose everything as well.

But my greatest pain was still not for me. Hearing statements like "Those gays say that they are born that way? True wickedness knows no bounds!" Or "To suggest God would create an abomination like a gay? Disgusting!" wounded me, and made me fearful. Still, I learned to survive. But what of the teenagers who heard such comments? How did those who were just beginning to confront their sexual desires make sense of such hatred?

I can see the progress in the larger culture, and be thankful for it.

At the same time, I can ask that you understand: that progress leaves me (and those like me) isolated, depressed, and in doubt. What can be done to reach those of us who are isolated and afraid? The talk of gay marriage, inclusion, and even respect for differing views means little to those of us trying to survive. I do not mean to sound selfish, but it is hard to rejoice over gay marriage when being outed could mean the loss of everything important to us.

"The love that dare not speak its name has become the love that won't shut up" is a quote attributed to Canadian author Robertson Davies.[2] With the acceptance accorded to sexual minorities in mainstream media and the emphasis on dialogue among several Christian denominations previously committed to a strong defense against sexual minorities,[3] it is easy to overlook the virulent opposition that continues.[4] Yet we need look no further than the controversy over Confederate monuments to find a violent clash of values, old and new, that continues unabated in America.[5] It should come as no surprise that those who have long held a fundamental Christian view continue to consider gays and those who are transgender immoral.

The overt Amish *attitude* toward gays is straightforward, without nuance or subtlety, as the narrative vignette that begins this chapter indicates. Same-sex sexual activity is a sin. As one Amish young man confirmed, gays are "the lowest of the low." He referenced, as does the vignette, those who choose to identify themselves as part of the queer community and act on their erotic desires with a same-sex partner.[6]

What is subtle, nuanced, and richly layered are Amish heteronormative attitudes toward the variety of same-sex behaviors that accompany (a) developmental stages, (b) emotional expressions of affection and even love, (c) the intimacy inherent in a collective culture, and (d) the place for same-sex relationships outside their culture, apoplectic indignation of the clergy notwithstanding. This chapter starts by exploring the controls imposed to ensure that gay social and political phenomena remains of the world.

The Revolution That Wasn't

In June of 1969, America faced another summer of angry demonstrations as the Vietnam War dragged on. No one anticipated that three nights of resistance from drag queens and down-and-out patrons at a bar in Greenwich Village called the Stonewall Inn would become the rallying point for a nascent movement by gays to assert their rights.[7] But civil rights movements are built on just such twists of fate, and the now-famous Stonewall rebellion was no exception. Rousted in what began as routine raids, these bored and disgruntled victims of what was then commonplace harassment threw rocks and bottles and danced in conga lines around the police attempting to arrest them. The rest, as they say, is history.

None of which mattered a whit to the Amish 150 miles south in Lancaster, Pennsylvania, or anywhere else on the North American continent. What mattered to them, at that point, was the status of conscientious objectors who were failing to return to their settlements following their stint of alternative service.[8] The behavior of degenerates in faraway New York City was of little concern, beyond condemning their immorality, on the farms or around the kitchen tables in the stolid homes of these Plain people.

The early gay liberation movement was spawned in the rumblings of the 1960s counterculture,[9] but it was assisted by an unlikely advocate in an unanticipated sphere. In 1970, Laud Humphreys published his dissertation research under the title *Tearoom Trade: Impersonal Sex in Public Places.*[10] Humphreys, a sociologist, researched the sexual behavior of males who met in public restrooms for anonymous sexual encounters. His book generated significant controversy and drove not only the issue of impersonal public sex, but also of same-sex behavior more generally, to the forefront in social scientific circles, the latter at the same time it was becoming a matter of heated public debate.

To fast forward, on June 26, 2015, in the matter of *Obergefell v. Hodges,* the U.S. Supreme Court upheld the validity of gay marriage, effectively closing a chapter on one of the hardest and longest fought struggles for same-sex legitimacy.[11] And the Amish? With regard to accepting same-sex behavior, their current attitude remains no different from that of those families living south of New York City as the early rumblings of discontent overflowed in 1969.

No matter where one stands on the moral and political veracity of the queer community, it is mind boggling to consider that the Amish have succeeded in avoiding any enmeshment in that sociopolitical firestorm for over fifty years. There are those who dive into Rumspringa on one end and sashay out the other, leaving plain clothing and Amish values behind. Others initially choose to join the Amish church, only later embracing an identity as members of the queer community.[12] To take the latter journey, however, as gay, lesbian, genderfluid, and transgender each has left their former culture. None decided to remain, stage a coup, and change the system, even by breaking away and creating a new affiliation of churches. The heteronormative expectation is sufficient to convince them to cut their ties, rather than initiate a social revolution. Standing outside the culture many are vocal critics, but they join the ranks of numerous other former Amish left to howl their protests at a fortress that is tightly shuttered against their advances.[13]

The reason for the church's success in discouraging the development of a gay Amish subgroup is simple. As noted previously, personal identity is subsumed to the group. If the personal clashes with the collective, it must either be relinquished or hidden, the latter decision accompanied by shame and guilt. As there is a limited set of confidantes, if any, with whom such feelings can be shared, there is no traction for forming a like-minded group of individuals willing to challenge the system from within. Power therefore remains with the collective, and the individual remains under its control.

I was once told of a police raid on a mobile home in which a number of Amish males, all of Rumspringa age, were found drunk and nude. Curious, I began a discrete round of inquiries and learned that the boys in question were probably a cadre of Amish youth who questioned their sexuality. (Later, several chose not to join the Amish church and acknowledged a gay sexual orientation.) Anxious to find a way to meet these sexual rebels, I spoke to a young man recently baptized who, I knew, was stepping away from a wild Rumspringa himself. He mentioned another baptized Amish man, in his mid-thirties and single, who was on good terms with one of these youngsters and could serve as a liaison.

"So, is —— gay?" I asked, referencing the identified potential liaison (and using "gay" in this context as shorthand for "he has same-sex feelings he would never act on because he's Amish"). The response was a frantic diatribe on the inappropriateness of the question, the demand that I not even hint at such a possibility to anyone else, and earnest pleas that this conversation immediately be forgotten. I apologized in a profuse, if scattershot, manner for my faux pas. "I'm sorry," I said. "But I just assumed that being Amish and not married in his mid-thirties, there was a good chance he was 'gay.'" My confidante bestowed a look that so eloquently said "Duh!" before uttering a word. "Of *course* he's gay!" he exclaimed. "But we don't talk about it!" This exchange demonstrates, once again, that community awareness, especially if the individual is well liked and well respected, does not translate to widespread condemnation. Instead, there is an effort to support that person in suppressing one's true sexual identity and presenting a heterosexual front to the collective culture.

This exchange demonstrates how the Amish, through their application of firm heteronormative expectations, avoid even the affirmative spark of a queer community in their midst. Those who experience such yearnings are welcome to stay, provided, as is true with paraphilias, that their desires remain a suppressed part of their personal identity and are limited by acceptable boundaries. If they cannot or choose not to do so, and fail to respond to church discipline, they are forced out.

Same-Sex Amish Desires

Many can empathize with those from families, and even cultures, in which their sexual desires are considered not only deviant, but evil.[14] It is more difficult to generalize empathy for those who have been raised in the environment of a collective culture that frowns on these desires, and to further understand the power of the mind in this cohesive, if not group-think atmosphere, to subvert these feelings. This is a process designed to suppress sexual desires and identity. It differs from a deliberate, manualized conversion therapy, a type of intervention to alter same-sex feelings that has been repeatedly demonstrated to have limited efficacy.[15] Many persons in the queer community recognize feeling different at an early age, but for those who struggle with same-sex longings, it is often during the onset of adolescence, as hormones create significant physiological changes, including a burgeoning sexual awareness, that the full enormity of this difference becomes apparent. It is also during this time that they begin the process of attempting to suppress unwanted desires.[16]

The outcome of any effort to suppress same-sex feelings varies, as the degree of success with conversion therapy attests.[17] Anecdotally, it seems as though the power of a collective culture is a mediating influence that substantially increases efficacy, at least for informal conversion efforts. Yet suppression is far from foolproof. Confessions of same-sex behavior are sufficiently common that they come as no surprise in Amish churches, an indication that these feelings do emerge and are acted out with relative frequency.[18] Despite these repeated transgressions, the number of Amish who leave the church and their families because they identify as a member of the queer community is small. Again, although the evidence is anecdotal, this suggests that the balance of community support and expectations, including a straight orientation, outweighs the benefits that identifying as a member of a sexual minority might bestow.

I once worked with a young Amish man who struggled at length with whether to endorse his same-sex feelings or join the Amish church. He eventually did join the church, marry, and is comfortably ensconced in his family. Still, he made an eloquent statement that neatly placed his dilemma in context. In a moment of wrenching vulnerability he said, "It would be wonderful to be in a same-sex relationship. But I would give up so much."

In the mainstream media and online, stories are rampant about persons who own their sexuality and come out in the face of familial opposition. They encounter hostility, anger, verbal abuse, and, at times, physical aggression because of their choice. Some are disowned, isolated from the love and care of family members, a breach that separates them from all they have known in the past. The spiritual path for those who embrace their same-sex desires is equally tumultuous, as many experience anger and feel betrayed by the religious backgrounds from which they emerge.[19]

A few among the Amish make this same choice. They break with all that they have known, opting to walk away from the collective "we" and strike out as an individual, identifying as a sexual minority. Many others choose a journey of sacrifice. Rather than allowing themselves to develop and act on these desires, they set them aside, living as they believe God has ordained. Were they grappling with a simple and uncomplicated paraphilia, a foot fetish perhaps, setting these desires aside would be an easier process. But in this case it is not. They renounce not just a sexual drive, a physical attraction. They also renounce the potential to develop relationships. These can be friendships, predicated on common interests as a sexual minority. Or they can be romantic liaisons, a fulfillment of the emotional desire that accompanies a physical interest.

Such individuals among the Amish sacrifice these potential rewards because they balance them against the loss of the collective culture. They would no longer be a part of their extended family, church, and settlement, all of which offer support and intimacy in ways that would never be regained. They would lose a fiscal safety net that remains in place so long as they commit themselves to the Amish church. Perhaps most important of all, they would walk away from an identity as God's chosen, with its undeniable understanding of right and wrong. They would step into a set of worldly values that, as they were taught, from cradle to grave, led away from the hope of an eternal life in heaven. They choose to remain with the Amish rather than "give up so much."

Still, the parameters of sexual identity are not as readily subsumed into cultural expectations as social and political identities that are modeled externally. Collective, heteronormative expectations can influence voting in governmental elections, membership in non-Amish organizations, and even a resistance to postmodern technology. These influences are ubiquitous. The Amish stand shoulder to shoulder not just with peers in the present, but also with an ancestry extending back over many generations. They will realize support yesterday, today, and tomorrow for these same beliefs. Yet that collective embrace forces Amish who are sexual minorities to reject a part of themselves that they long to claim. There is marginal support, at best, for an internal struggle with transgender desires, or with same-sex longings. A wise community member knows that even the existence of such struggles is best kept hidden, unless one chooses to leave the Amish fold. No decision can be made that does not involve severe emotional pain. The narrative opening the chapter is a raw expression of this statement.

The Amish revulsion for same-sex activity is rooted in the fundamental expectation that sex occurs for the primary purpose of procreation. Both same-sex behavior and zoophilia are prohibited in the Books of Law in the Old Testament, so the greater anathema for same-sex activity, as opposed to sex with animals, at first seems incongruous. Paul and at least one New Testament book attributed to James also include verses that can be interpreted as denouncing the sin of same-sex behavior. Therefore, this particular failing is mentioned under both the old and new covenants.[20] In addition, there is a more pragmatic reason to look askance at same-sex dalliances. They have the potential to erode the hierarchy of the culture, as the long-established pattern of female submission does not account for the equal status of same-sex intimate partners. Likewise, acceptance of transgender persons plays havoc with the power of the patriarchy. Sin may create a distance from God with little reference to its degree, but sexual minorities threaten the heteronormative in ways other sins do not.

It Isn't Sex . . . but It's Close

There is one period in Amish life in which same-sex activity, while not condoned, is integrated and compartmentalized into a developmental phase. It is a recognized aspect of behavior in several settlements in Indiana and occurs in at least some areas of Pennsylvania and Ohio. Amish discomfort in acknowledging this particular activity makes it difficult to assess how widespread the practice may be, but it seems sufficiently commonplace to be widely known.

The behavior is subsumed into a game called "cows and bulls" (briefly discussed in chapter 2). As the name implies, young adolescent males assume the role of a "cow" or a "bull." They either simulate sexual activities or, for some, engage in actual anal intercourse. There appears to be a hierarchy in terms of social status as to whether a boy assumes an active or passive role. Other forms, such as oral sex or mutual masturbation, are relatively rare accompaniments, although they do occur. (There are reports of less formalized adolescent same-sex experimentation between males at this stage, as well as experimentation involving females only, and both genders.)[21]

The game has less to do with sexual attraction per se, and more with social dominance. The Amish value, and also teach, humility, but this game emerges at the confluence of a flood of hormones and an adolescent's effort to establish a personal identity.[22] Hormonal drives and the need for a sense of self run contrary to the humility these children are taught from the cradle. Mimicking the dominance pattern in the domesticated animals they observe across their lifetime serves as a means of establishing a hierarchy in their peer group, one that can be created away from the watchful and disciplining eyes of adults. If some of these youngsters find that the game satisfies a longing beyond the physical need and also resonates with emotional needs, that is an unintended perk. It opens the door to confusion and indecision as they decide whether to accept their sexual orientation or suppress it and join the church.[23]

The game does involve same-sex behavior and is a form of sexual acting out. Despite this, it occurs in a discrete period of childhood, to be later left behind, and is reluctantly acknowledged by most participants. (I have literally shut down an interview by making the mistake of referencing its existence in a freewheeling discussion of Amish sexual behavior.) Its far-flung presence, despite a heteronormative that forbids such activity, would suggest that it is a common developmental occurrence, albeit one that generates conflicting emotions. It may serve an important role in assigning feelings of guilt and remorse to same-sex activity, emotions that carry forward as these youths assume roles of leadership in the patriarchy.

Yet this discussion of adolescent sexuality has a glaring omission—females. As girls emerge into early adolescence, they, too, struggle with hormonal changes and the sexual urges that accompany them. The model of sexuality placed before them from earliest childhood continues. Their role is secondary to males. As such, they do not engage in sexual games that determine their social status. They explore sexuality, but in a less pressured manner than their male peers. The heteronormative expectation for Amish women does not center around authority, as is also true in the larger, traditional culture.[24] Thus their exploration does not carry that competitive edge prevalent in early adolescent male sexual play.

Whether male or female, early adolescent sexual exploration, combined with expanding options for gender roles, opens the door to more complex and nuanced relationships. It seems probable that the Amish reluctance to engage in critical thinking on issues such as sexual behavior assists them in compartmentalizing this particular period in their lives and allows them to frame these acts as being discrete in time and purpose.

Sexual Minorities and Marriage

As discussed in the chapter on intimacy, Amish closeness differs from that in the mainstream culture. Theirs is a trust and bond built on a collective. The mainstream emphasizes independent and autonomous individuals and is more likely to build trust on, and establish bonds with, smaller social units. Thus the power and control a culture exerts over sexuality is not confined to the sexual act itself, but to the manner in which intimacy is understood and carried out.

The traits that inform an Amish primary relationship, which will ultimately become a lifetime marriage, parallel those in the larger culture. Amish cultural concerns, however, carry a weight that the mainstream does not anticipate when considering the importance of romance, cohabitation, or marriage. The involvement of extended family, the church, and the settlement creates an intimacy that assumes far greater proportions. If struggles as a sexual minority, for either a husband or a wife, are acted out, they fall into the domain of the larger group.

The extent to which premarital disclosures are made, heard, and understood varies. At an early point in a couple's relationship, for the partner who identifies in any way as a sexual minority, this means choosing to take information that has been held in secret, a dramatic choice in a collective culture, and place it into greater public awareness, without a clear assurance of how that information will be received. Does a fiancé turn to his father, or a fiancée to her mother, opening a possible line of communication extending much farther than that cozy and discrete romantic partnership? Will the information be enough to end the potential nuptials? Or will it become a confidence and a struggle shared only between husband and wife? For some, it is easier to marry without revealing such secrets and allow the truth to unfold over time—if at all.

As noted earlier, a person's decision to join the church is often made in tandem with a contemplated marriage.[25] If a person struggling as a sexual minority becomes disillusioned, whether to remain, conflicted but embracing the Amish, or walk away is a choice that can involve not only membership in the church and the community, but also a life partner and children. To separate from a spouse means leaving the relationship in a much more complex way than the act of divorce. However tangled and unfulfilling aspects of that union might be, it is assumed to be a lifelong commitment within the collective society.

The emotional strain of relinquishing life with a spouse and ongoing involvement with one's children is expanded to include disengagement from the relationships that compose a community. It can be a long, long walk out that door and into the unknown. The influence of the group can neither be denied nor ignored when considering the choices of sexual minorities within Amish culture.

The Uneasy Truce

It bears repeating once again: to speak of "the" Amish as a single affiliation is to court disaster. There is no flat, categorical statement that describes the Amish attitude toward sexual minorities both within and outside the culture. The stories included in this chapter give a sense of their disdain for sexual minorities in the world and a hesitancy to recognize these persons within their group. The following two vignettes further refine an understanding of the way in which the Amish manage same-sex attraction with regard to their cultural boundaries.

In one, a minister was made aware that I was gay and took offense that I would counsel the Amish. We had known each other for years and worked cooperatively in the past. Accordingly, we met to see if there was a way to resolve the impasse. Our dialogue took a surprising turn. He shared that several years previously, he met an old friend while visiting in the Lancaster area. They spent several hours conversing, for they had been raised in the same church and were extremely close through early adulthood. As the pair reminisced, the minister found himself troubled. He vividly recalled their early adolescent games of cows and bulls. In the course of the conversation, which became intense and intimate on so many topics, his friend refused to discuss that aspect of their relationship, despite strong hints from the minister. In speaking with me, the minister's voice dropped, and he described the emotional bond the two had shared, their overnights together, and the intimacy that formed as they passed through this phase of development. His friend's resistance to revisiting these memories was puzzling and painful. He was deeply hurt as they said their good-byes once again.

I had not been asked to function as a counselor, and it was neither my place nor my purpose to explore the significance of his feelings. He still held tightly to the cultural rubric that deemed same-sex involvement a grievous sin, and he made that clear in our talk. But beliefs are thoughts, and thoughts can become tangled with the heart. The minister was describing, not just the loss of a meaningful romance, but also the pain of having that relationship dismissed. My only course was to silently empathize with his pain, since we were not allowed to name what he was sharing. That he was able to broach the topic at all was telling. Being English and gay myself, I would not judge the behavior he described. I was a confidante who would not exist inside his tightly structured community.

Another example highlights an Amish response when a threat to the community is only marginal. (This personal experience has been described in greater detail elsewhere).[26] A best-selling author and pundit spent a day with me interviewing several Amish for his next project. I had minor qualms, in that he was openly gay in his writings and, based on what I had seen on YouTube and in other media outlets, his presence left little question about his sexuality. Still, I believed that I could maneuver him to a series of potential interviews with individuals who would be willing to overlook his flamboyance. Among others whom we visited, I took him to the home of an Amish man in his mid-thirties. I had known this gentleman since he was in his early twenties, shortly after he joined the church. He was bright, articulate, and, because of a Rumspringa that took him deeper into the world than some of his peers, more streetwise than many in his community.

The author was chameleon-like—charming, attentive, and amazing in his ability to extract information. At one point he excused himself to use the restroom, leaving my Amish confidante alone with me. My friend fashioned a sly grin and, referencing the writer, asked, "Gay?" "Yep," I replied. There was a moment to ponder this revelation, and my friend next asked, "Christian?" "He's an atheist," I replied. There was a longer moment of reflection, and then my friend laughed. "I wish I could tell someone other than my wife about this. It's such a unique situation. An Amish man talking with a gay atheist."

The author returned, the interview continued, and it eventually ended on a warm note of appreciation. My Amish friend brought the author on a tour through his home, taking time to show him where church would be held in their barn the following Sunday, as well as the bench wagon parked in the back drive, which held the seats and hymnals that accompanied the service as it moved from house to house. In this setting, the presence of an openly gay individual, who was also an atheist, did not perturb an Amish man. The purpose of the interaction did not impact the community. The heteronormative expectations of the culture were not threatened.

Do these vignettes suggest an easing of the rigid boundaries that form the Amish heteronormative's expectations toward sexual minorities? In all probability, no. These were individuals with whom I had established relationships. In the case of the minister, there was tension, but there was also a longstanding history from which to address his concerns. Facing outward from their culture and interacting with a liberal English confidante, both Amish men felt the freedom to explore outside the boundaries of the heteronormative. Facing inward toward their culture, each would doubtless assume an attitude of heavy-handed disapproval regarding sexual minorities.

The Internal and External Pressures of Same-Sex Desires

The Amish are far from immune to worldly influences, and the same-sex "wolf at the door" continues to be perceived as howling for its fellow wolves to join the hedonistic and hell-bound pack. Amish leaders are aware of their own members who struggle with same-sex feelings and deem it important to remind them that such feelings are unacceptable. The subtle networks through which Amish gays, lesbians, and those who are transgender find each other within their culture are the same types of networks used across so many cultures when discretion is necessary to communicate a desire.[27] The power that any culture holds can limit the development of a social network, but it fails to control the behavior of those it purports to manage.

What occurs once a person initially opts to no longer remain among the Amish? The struggle to share with family that one is a sexual minority can consume as much time as making the decision to leave does. If the choice to separate is arrived at prior to joining the church, the reason for the departure can be kept discrete. The degree of acceptance varies by family, church, and settlement, but it almost always includes at least a chill in relationships. The culture one once knew is gone.[28]

The increasing acceptance of and tolerance for sexual minorities in the mainstream culture makes the struggle harder for those ensconced in the Amish fold and its heteronormative view. Their choice, however, is not simply to come out and accept a true sexual orientation. It includes the decision to renounce a collective identity as paramount in favor of a personal sense of self. To better empathize with this, imagine for a moment making the decision to renounce one's family, career, all material possessions, and all future plans. Instead, the choice is to invest fully in the hopes, dreams, and beliefs of a spiritual group that maintains an enormous measure of control over one's life, while renouncing the spiritual beliefs with which this individual was raised. In a cultural reverse, this is what Amish persons embracing their sexual minority status are asked to do.

And what happens for those who leave? Consider the demands placed upon an Amish individual who embraces an identity as a sexual minority and steps out into the world. Sexual minority status is, by its definition, an autonomous role, one not subject to the rule or control of another. Someone who has been taught to live in a collective culture is asked to make the transition not just to the freedom of independence, but also to one of the least-supported positions that the heteronormative mainstream can provide. Piled on to the other adjustments that must be made in moving from Amish to English life, sexual minority status vastly increases the pressures a former Amish individual faces.

The Amish heteronormative can be viewed as homophobic, although sexually stigmatizing may be a more accurate description.[29] It seems important to place this current pushback in its cultural context. The Amish respond to perceived threats to their culture with an implacable unconcern for perceptions from the world. Throughout the fifty years that the equality of sexual minorities has been increasing, there has been relatively little response by the Amish church. It is only since the advent of gay marriage that their clergy became truly alarmed. As sexual minorities find a seat at the mainstream table, they pose a threat that did not previously exist.

As of this writing, we are not currently on a major war footing. Yet there are still those in Amish leadership positions who recall the efforts to protect their culture when members who served as conscientious objectors were exposed to the world.[30] I recall a conversation with a former Amish man who was a child in Indiana during World War II. Because Amish schoolchildren were nonresistant, they could not participate in public school activities to support the war effort or pledge allegiance to the flag. He and his Amish schoolmates were ridiculed and bullied by what were perceived as their more patriotic peers. In context, the Amish attempt to maintain their heteronormative standard is part of a larger, longstanding, overarching effort to retain their way of life, regardless of the derision heaped upon them. There is no evidence that external pressure will create change. Sexual minorities remain a clouded issue for the Amish, one that will doubtless continue to be a troubling social concern for the foreseeable future.

Epilogue

Rubbing Shoulders with Rahab

Emerging Views on Sexuality

One of the subtle markers of change among the Amish can be found with Rumspringa-age youth in Shipshewana, Indiana. There, boys often work hard to appear non-Amish in their dress. Over the years, in visiting that area, I usually stop at the convenience store in the center of town before heading home. It is one of the few places open late, and I have braved the cold and tracked wet snow across the tile floor, or wished for a cool breeze as the summer heat still sweltered in the night. Almost always, a few young men were there, too, sharing that nervous camaraderie of late adolescence. At first it was easy to spot the Amish among them. We would stand in line at the counter under the glare of fluorescent lights, nameless customers in an anonymous store. No matter how good their disguise, no matter how well they blended into the scene, the smell of "white gas," or lantern fuel, wafted from the clothes of these dancers on the devil's playground.[1] And now, as the years pass by? I still brave the cold, or wish for a cool breeze. But within those Plain homes dotting the landscape, batteries have become the norm. Only churches that cling to the most conservative Ordnungs still insist on lighting by lanterns. It takes a subtler cue than that telltale petroleum odor to know the young man waiting his turn in line is, in reality, steeped in a culture so different from mine. Change comes slowly. But change does come.

The Amish recognize the inevitable and necessary role of the world in their lives. The title of this epilogue references the prostitute Rahab, mentioned in the Old Testament as plying her trade in the streets of Jericho.[2] She offered information and advice to the spies sent by the Israelite commander, Joshua, and assisted him in conquering her city. She is also listed in the lineage of Christ.[3] The story is a reminder that the heteronormative ideal in any culture is built on universal human needs. As both queer theory and the story of Rahab remind us, sex and power are inextricably linked.

A question arises as the Amish slowly, slowly, adapt to the world that surrounds them and permeates their lives. Despite their intransigence, will the day come when they wed Mr. and Mr. Yoder? The famous wit and author Dorothy Parker has said, "If you wear a short enough skirt, the party will come to you." But this is exactly what the Amish do not want, so presumably both their metaphorical and actual skirts (at least on the women) will remain very, very long. As the world stokes the fires of hell, they will keep the heat at bay, hewing to their traditions and maintaining a rigid, frigid (or at least collective and high-context) view of morality.

Sexuality and the Amish: The Past and the Present

The Amish heteronormative functions on the basis of spiritual and cultural mandates. Their spiritual mandate flows from three core Anabaptist beliefs.[4] One, they dispute human reason as the foundation for knowledge. Two, they question personal autonomy as a source of freedom or happiness. Three, they dismiss the merits of moral relativity. Each of these beliefs is affirmed in their views on sex and sexuality. In looking beyond worldly logic, emphasizing the collective, and standing firm on moral principles, they pursue the hope of eternal life in the presence of God. To embrace the temporality of this world is self-centered and short sighted.

In the *ideal*, spiritual and cultural mandates are synonymous. In application, they overlap to varying degrees. The term "cultural Catholic" is used to describe those who identify with the Catholic church but have a minimal investment in it.[5] The term "cultural Amish" could describe some who identify with this collective and high-context culture. A commitment to maintaining the heteronormative ensures their role in a stable system, but their concern with the spiritual purpose behind that system is lacking. Regardless, the spiritual and the cultural strive to maintain boundaries against intrusions from the world.

While feminist advances would seem to be the greatest threat to the patriarchy, the Amish have parried that thrust with minimal difficulty.[6] Women in Amish churches that engage in greater interaction with mainstream culture, such as Beachy Amish and Fellowship churches, require a more submissive role for women than churches that maintain a greater distance, suggestive of one mechanism to ensure that heteronormative values remain undisturbed.[7] Still, the Amish have long experience in observing evolving roles for women.[8] In what is described as a soft patriarchy,[9] females submit to males with the understanding that this stance is flexible and, at times, egalitarian. Therefore, vertical hierarchical movement in feminine roles is common, albeit not rising to the level of consistent equality found in the mainstream.

Recently, the role of women among the Amish does seem to be experiencing a groundswell. They are contributing more to the financial success of the household. Freedom during Rumspringa is also greater, as certain settlements report females purchasing vehicles. Women in other settlements have a greater sense of comfort in a role as single adult, with less emphasis attached to becoming a wife and mother. Indirect evidence also indicates the more frequent use of contraception. While this may be a shared decision between husband and wife, historically it implies greater freedom for the female partner. Despite these changes, it seems that the Amish have little to fear from feminism.

Then again, perhaps they do. Evolving views enter virtually every culture through the young, who see the least to lose in changing the system. Parker's "short skirt" has already arrived in the form of the cell phone and its insidious access to the internet. The far-reaching presence of this technology, even in the most conservative settlements,[10] means that a discrete portal to the world is open for virtually all Amish. Similar to the Indiana bishop's fears for an Amish child in foster care (chapter 7), it takes only one "world traveler," sharing the information obtained online from a cell phone with family and friends, for the damage to be done. And Amish youngsters, rest assured, are already well aware of this information superhighway, including the exits that lead straight to porn.

But it is more than pornography that these young people enjoy. When I first began working with the Amish, a daring few would appear at a movie theater, taking in a show and eating popcorn during their brief time in Rumspringa. Now, movies stream continuously on their phones. Not only can they view dramas, adventures, and comedies, but also the accompanying interpretations of ways in which men and women relate. The power and control of the collective loosens its grip as the entertainment industry gives them a front row seat to patterns of interaction that could formerly only be observed from afar. Like almost every other North American, they are learning social mores from the media. Unless they consciously hold themselves to a steady stream of films from the 1950s and earlier, primary values such as the submissive role of women, nonresistance in the face of war, and resistance to technology are at risk of being eroded from within as these adolescents access cell phones in privacy.[11]

Are their values as tenuous as this bleak outlook assumes? Amish youth also sit for three hours on a Sunday in worship with their neighbors and families. They listen as the bishop and the ministers preach earnestly and, at times, verge on passion, sharing the higher purpose of our sojourn on earth and the dangers of the world that surrounds them. They remain encapsulated by family, by neighbors who double as the church, and by settlements that remind them on a daily, hourly, even minute-by-minute basis that they are Amish and therefore not of the world. Dress, deportment, work, language, and interpersonal interactions all reinforce that they are a peculiar people, separated from those who are godless.

Who will win their hearts? Such a question naïvely assumes that there are no Amish females sporting chauvinistically named "tart

art" (discreetly applied tattoos—there are), Amish males with hafada piercings (in the scrotum—there are), and a hundred other acting-out behaviors that occur just below the waterline (a terrible pun—it is), the better to remain unnoticed by a hierarchy that would signal its vehement displeasure if it only knew. Whether the young will reinvent the heteronormative based on their exposure to other influences remains to be seen. Still, even if feminism increases its challenge, it is a demand for egalitarian gender roles. The slow change for which the Amish are known buys time for the patriarchy.

A more distressing risk is the intrusion of civil authority. While spiritual and cultural mandates overlap, they are not identical. If governmental agencies are allowed too much oversight into Amish affairs, the freedom to practice their beliefs is lost. The religious custom of using lay midwives to safeguard women from exposure to hospitals is a matter that could eventually find its way to state or even federal appeals courts. What is considered to be the encroachment of state agencies to protect children who have been sexually abused has less merit as an argument, but such outside involvement more directly impacts the authority of the patriarchy.

The Amish do not condone child sexual abuse. It is deplored both inside and outside of Amish culture. But the Amish prefer to be the primary source of discipline for perpetrators and of response to the victims. Theirs is a strong belief in suffering being inherent in life.[12] They also adhere to the need for forgiveness. These principles create a much different heteronormative than the legal system allows. Parsing blame, accepting confessions, and offering forgiveness must occur within the church, as well as within the Amish social order. Civil authorities fail to understand the essential nature of this process. In addition, the comparative power of their authority weakens the patriarchy in the eyes of its membership. For these spiritual and practical reasons, the Amish maintain an ongoing resistance to external participation in these matters.

Still, such challenges to the heteronormative pale in comparison with the threat of sexual freedom. This becomes so severe because it emerges from within and is championed from without. Particularly for those Amish who experience longings consistent with a sexual minority, the mainstream increasingly offers support. Return for a moment to the comment made by the young man who struggled with same-sex desires. "It would be wonderful to be in a same-sex relationship, but I would give up so much." Make a substitution for the phrase "be in a same-sex relationship"—"divorce," "marry the non-Amish person I truly want to marry," or even "live together before we take the step to commit to marriage"—and the sentence still fits. In each case, all who either join the Amish church or contemplate doing so recognize that they are choosing to accept a tight-knit community that can, at times, offer stifling oversight and discipline, but also provides security against the loneliness, existential uncertainty, and financial deprivation taken for granted as a necessary part of life in the mainstream. The control the culture wields over sexual behavior is balanced by the perks it provides as a collective group.

Yet it is easier to renounce socially based decisions than longings of the heart. Same-sex or transgender feelings are psychological and emotional experiences that well up from within. (So, for that matter, is falling in and out of love, but the struggle of whether and how to stay or go in relationships is a universal conundrum beyond the scope of this text.) These desires can be challenged by the culture, but gay marriage is legal. Medical procedures to enhance gender conformity are accessible. There are tantalizing messages from the mainstream, assuring these individuals that who they are, *as* they are, or as they want to be, is acceptable. This view of an unfiltered identity, at odds with the collective, is a tempting Siren's song.

How, then, do those who identify as a sexual minority adjust to life within their culture? Amish identity is centered on the community. Acceptance of a minority status would defy the heteronormative. This does not suggest a lack of sense of self. For the overwhelming majority, each has a solid identity as a unique individual. The goals of that unique self are focused on serving, nurturing, and maintaining the community. A collective cultural expectation is ingrained in their existential purpose. To this end, the heteronormative expectations of the culture are to be respected. This includes an understanding of sexual behavior as being primarily for procreation. Every member overtly respects the patriarchal hierarchy, with its Ordnung, as offering a structure that both disciplines and nurtures. To be gay or transgender, or in any other way embrace a sexual minority status, falls outside that norm.

The Amish emphasize the utility of all behaviors as a means of glorifying God. Sexual activity as an act of reproduction is both natural and utilitarian, an expenditure of energy that falls within the natural order. For two persons of the same sex, or a person who has changed gender surgically, to engage in sexual activity is to do so for pleasurable purposes only, with no hope of conception. (Heterosexual couples who are unable to conceive are at least within the broad parameters of God's plan.) To condone sex solely as a pleasurable act endorses hedonism. It would require a seismic shift in Amish thinking to tolerate such a change in position.

These sexual minorities also risk undermining the patriarchy, a further practical risk. A soft patriarchy? That is possible. A patriarchy in which men partner with men, women with women, and genders are capable of change? Not possible at all. Beyond any spiritual basis for this fire bell in the night, it is a reality-based threat to the authority and government that has held sway since the church was founded. Still, what will be the long-term response as sexual minorities insinuate themselves into Amish life? While no one can predict the future with certainty, the past holds at least some clues.

Sexuality and the Amish: The Future

Contrast Amish identity with that of the American and Canadian mainstream. In the latter culture, identity is individualized, as each person seeks to make a statement that is unique. Teamwork is not perceived as subsuming one's identity with others, but as integrating separate ideas and concepts to create a novel solution. The social ideal is increasingly egalitarian across genders and sexual minorities. Yet social scientists are concerned that, instead of increasing sociability, social media isolates individuals.[13] At times the Amish heteronormative appears a throwback to mid-twentieth-century American and Canadian values. While parallels of reserving sexual activity for marriage and limiting a woman's role spring from the same Judeo-Christian ethic, just as the North American mainstream has evolved, so has the heteronormative within the collective and high-context Amish culture.

In fairness, to view the world from an Amish perspective, they have not generated a John Wayne Gacy, a Ted Bundy, or a Jeffrey Dahmer to terrorize humanity as serial killers with a sexually sadistic twist. They remained unfazed as the HIV/AIDS epidemic cut a swath through the gay community before settling into a socioeconomic crisis.[14] As their third largest state of residence faced a crisis in its child welfare system, due to chronic underfunding in the face of an ever-increasing demand for services related to neglected and abused children, the Amish took care of their own.[15] From behind the castle walls of Amish beliefs, the surrounding countryside can look bleak indeed.

The Amish offer a startling contrast to the postmodern view of sexuality and gender roles. As this book has demonstrated, the heteronormative within their culture remains based on a unifying principle, an understanding of sexuality as emerging from a divine plan. As a high-context and collective culture, there is no need to determine another individual's viewpoint on the role of women, the purpose of sex, or gay marriage. These opinions are already known, at least in so far as they will be shared at the social level. Consider again the vignette that begins the preface. The deacon made a conscious choice in joining the church. He rejected the option to support individual identities that emerged into the mainstream fifty years ago with the Stonewall rebellion and allowed him to guard the women's restroom while a transgender friend made a social statement. Instead, he joined a collective identity that began five hundred years ago with the Anabaptist rebellion, and he now stands in solidarity with his brothers and sisters who commit to a narrower but commonly held view of sexual expression.

It would be too easy to mistake this Amish viewpoint for a reticence that keeps them grounded in a midcentury view of sexuality and gender roles. As queer theory demonstrates, however, the heteronormative is influenced both by group norms and external pressures imposed on these norms. The Amish view is molded and shaped in part by mainstream social forces. Their stance must accordingly change to accommodate the pressures that push against it. It is the power of the collective, however, that allows them to do so successfully.

Yet there are tantalizing clues as to how further change may occur. "Collective" does not equate with "lockstep." The all-encompassing term "the" Amish does not apply, in large part because affiliations have separated, due to disagreements over the appropriate application of the Ordnung. The founder of current studies of the Amish, John A. Hostetler, writes of his father's excommunication over just such a dispute.[16] Doubtless this event encouraged his analysis of the culture. Still another case study describes the fall from grace of a bishop over the introduction of kerosene refrigerators.[17] These are anecdotal incidents, each involving one person. Yet they are also a microcosm of the effort to maintain rules and standards that has led, over time, to the formation of multiple affiliations and separate groups identifying themselves with the Amish name.

What is likely to occur, then, beginning in isolated church districts and expanding from there, is a tolerance toward those who engage in what are now rejected sexual practices. This is highly unlikely to be a widespread and in-depth social change. Still, there may be a lessening of the stigmas attached to certain behaviors. A gradual and grudging acknowledgement of various types of interactions. A resignation to the state of the world that surrounds them. These church districts will fall out of affiliation with many others around them, but align with some who are gradually evolving to accept a similar set of beliefs. As these churches lose and gain affiliations, it is possible for yet another group or groups, identified as Amish, to emerge from this redistribution with differing heteronormative ideals.

Change comes slowly, but change does come. Nonetheless, it happens at a pace that they dictate. The marriage of Mr. and Mr. Yoder? Or the presentation of Mrs. Schwartz, surgically changed from Mr. Schwartz? Not at any time soon. Dissolution of the Amish? Also unlikely. They have grappled with tough choices in the past and demonstrated their enduring character. In the future? They can face the changing moral structure that surrounds them with grace, strength, and equanimity.

Appendix A

Suggestions for Further Reading

For those readers new to the Amish, the following books are a useful starting point to better understand this Plain people.

The Amish, by Donald B. Kraybill, Karen M. Johnson-Weiner, and Steven M. Nolt (Baltimore: Johns Hopkins University Press, 2013). This definitive, twenty-two chapter book provides a comprehensive overview of Amish life and culture in North America. While scholarly and meticulous, it is still written in an accessible style.

The Amish: A Concise Introduction, by Steven M. Nolt (Baltimore: Johns Hopkins University Press, 2016). This is a compact portrait of present-day Amish society. It is an excellent choice for the reader who wants an understanding of Amish history and background in context but does not need in-depth historical information.

Amish Grace: How Forgiveness Transcended Tragedy, by Donald B. Kraybill, Steven M. Nolt, and David Weaver-Zercher (San Francisco: Jossey-Bass, 2007). This is a narrative of the Nickel Mines shootings, in which a gunman held ten Amish schoolgirls hostage, killing five. The world was riveted by the Amish willingness to forgive. The authors recount the tragedy and explain the dynamics of Amish culture that allowed this unselfish response.

An Amish Paradox: Diversity and Change in the World's Largest Amish Community, by Charles E. Hurst and David L. McConnell (Baltimore: Johns Hopkins University Press, 2010). The authors explore both the continuity and change of Amish values and practices within the large Amish community in the Holmes County, Ohio, settlement.

The Amish Way: Patient Faith in a Perilous World, by Donald Kraybill, Steven M. Nolt, and David Weaver-Zercher (San Francisco: Jossey-Bass, 2010). This introduction to Amish religion and spirituality interprets their worldview as well as specific faith practices.

Growing Up Amish: The Rumspringa Years, second edition, by Richard A. Stevick (Baltimore: Johns Hopkins University Press, 2014). His book explores the transitional stage of Amish life between childhood and an ultimate assimilation into the community from its social, cultural, and psychological aspects.

A History of the Amish, third edition, by Steven M. Nolt (New York: Good Books, 2015). Written in a readable and engaging style, this thorough history traces the Amish from their Anabaptist roots in Europe through the present.

Plain Diversity: Amish Cultures and Identities, by Steven M. Nolt and Thomas J. Meyers (Baltimore: Johns Hopkins University Press, 2007). This is a specific examination of nineteen Amish settlements in Indiana, focusing on the diversity found there and the impact of these differences on Amish life and interactions.

The Riddle of Amish Culture, revised edition, by Donald B. Kraybill (Baltimore: Johns Hopkins University Press, 2001). A classic work, explaining the effort to negotiate with modernity that led Amish culture to its present status.

Train Up a Child: Old Order Amish and Mennonite Schools, by Karen M. Johnson-Weiner (Baltimore: Johns Hopkins University Press, 2010). This explores the ideological principles underlying private schools among the Amish, explaining in depth the pedagogy, curriculum, textbooks, and even school design that all serve to maintain the dominant influence of the community and separate these children from the world.

Appendix B

Professional Interaction
and Amish Sexuality

The question of how best to respect Amish beliefs about sexual behavior, sexuality, and gender roles applies to those in the helping professions, law enforcement, the judiciary, and social scientists. While posed as a question of respecting *their* beliefs, a second question lurks behind. How best to ask the Amish to respect *our* beliefs about sexual behavior, sexuality, and gender roles? A basic awareness of Amish expectations and behavior guides interactions in both directions.

Descriptions of Amish culture center on terms such as "collective society" and "high context." Their focus on the group minimizes the importance of the individual in their lives, in comparison with the more autonomous mainstream. Their emphasis on small social units (family, church, settlement) enhances a specific intimacy between individuals. There is far less concern for overarching bureaucracy or organizational structure.

As an outgrowth of this cultural system, the Amish care far less, for example, that a deputy is a member of a specific county sheriff's department. They care more that he is "Deputy Miller." They are less interested in whether a physician has privileges at a specific hospital or is employed there. What counts is that she is "Dr. Graber." A social worker has little standing because she is employed by the county. She gains status as the community learns that she is "Mrs. Johns."

In the same way, the Amish are less concerned about political affiliations, social involvement, or activism. (The quiet but steady infiltration of self-help groups into their culture has been one exception.) An individual's interpersonal style, one's manner of relating to the Amish, is far more important than political beliefs or efforts to obtain social justice. As the Amish learn to appreciate the people with whom they are working, a saying they apply comes to the fore: "We don't care how much you know until we know how much you care." It is the genuineness, the compassion, and the interpersonal style of the individual that decides whether she or he is accepted.

For example, I have observed an Amish bishop teasing and joking with a young man wheeling him out of the hospital. It was impossible not to observe the tattoos wending their way up that staff member's arms and under his scrubs, or the holes in his ears, nose, eyebrows, and lip where piercings would obviously be replaced when he was off duty. I knew a driver in one Amish settlement who was careful not to mention his boyfriend and discretely removed the rainbow flag adorning his rearview mirror when serving the Amish, but otherwise was well known. Couples cohabitating, women who terminated their pregnancies, untold numbers of divorced and remarried souls, all interact with the Amish without obvious censure. Religious background, current involvement, voting record, or social views will not be a primary consideration in whether to engage with an individual.

At the same time it is important to realize that the Amish do *not* practice moral relativism. From time to time I hear a comment on how open the Amish are to differing beliefs. My own experience has been that they are reluctant to criticize (or, in their opinion, judge) beliefs that are different from theirs. This does not mean that they agree with or would tolerate in their own community beliefs that outsiders hold. I have observed warm, caring relationships between the Amish and service providers in the mainstream that exist despite firmly held differences of opinion regarding politics, social issues, religion, or spirituality. The expression of these differences is muted, as the Amish perceive no need to create a challenge to others by expressing their beliefs. Yet it would be a mistake to consider the lack of a rebuff as a sign of diffidence for an opposing view.

For those who anticipate and need a genuine acceptance of morality different from the conservative and traditional views held by the Amish, disappointment awaits. They will respect but not accept alternate views. For those equally committed to a set of opposing values (for example. the right of all women to freedom of choice and equality, or the right of sexual minorities to express themselves in all cultures) imposing these values on the Amish fails to respect them and their beliefs. With the deep divide that often exists between professionals and the Amish, if open dialogue is not possible, the best approach may be a recognition that silence on both sides signals a respect for the values of the other.

For those seeking further information on working with the Amish, my earlier work addresses services to this population by the helping professions. It is *Serving the Amish: A Cultural Guide for Professionals*, by James A. Cates (Baltimore: Johns Hopkins University Press, 2014).

Appendix C

A Quick Guide to Other Plain Groups

Anabaptist affiliations have surged and declined over the centuries since the movement emerged during the Protestant Reformation in sixteenth-century Europe. In the twenty-first century, four major branches flourish. The Amish, Brethren, Hutterites, and Mennonites continue this tradition. Because of their distinctive plain dress, Amish and Hutterites are sometimes referred to as Plain people. There are also contingents of more-traditional plain-dressing people within the Brethren and Mennonite groups, as well as a few other plain-dressing look-alikes who deserve mention.

Brethren

Originally called German Baptist Brethren, this sect was nicknamed "Dunkers" or "Dunkards" for their practice of adult baptism by immersion. Emerging in Germany in the early 1700s, the Brethren are a branch grafted onto the Anabaptist tree, because their theology was strongly influenced by the beliefs and practices of both radical Pietism and Anabaptists. Numerous North American Brethren groups trace their roots to these early German origins.

Most Brethren no longer wear plain clothing, but a traditional subgroup, known as the Old German Baptist Brethren, can be confused with the Amish. They dress in distinctive plain clothing, and the men grow beards. Another group, the Old Order River Brethren (a traditional community within the Brethren in Christ denomination), are very similar to the Old German Baptist Brethren in appearance, with their plain clothing and beards. Both groups allow motorized vehicles, electricity from the grid, higher education, and limited use of online services.

Hutterites

This group descends directly from the early Anabaptist movement. While the Amish are a collective culture in that they emphasize social and emotional reliance on the group, the Hutterites are collective in that they practice economic communalism. The Hutterites reject private property and cluster in rural colonies composed of approximately one hundred individuals (both adults and children). They wear distinctive dress, but, unlike the Amish, they fully embrace high technology, owned and operated communally. Their name derives from one of their early leaders, Jakob Hutter, a martyr who was burned alive as a heretic in the mid-1500s. In twenty-first-century North America, they have some five hundred colonies, the majority in the Canadian provinces of Alberta, Manitoba, and Saskatchewan, and a smaller number in South Dakota and Montana.

Mennonites

"Mennonite" is an umbrella term for more than 150 different groups in North America, with a European lineage in Switzerland, Germany, Austria, France, and the Netherlands. Beginning in the last half of the twentieth century, their churches have seen an increasing ethnic diversity that includes Asian and Hispanic members. Like the Brethren, most Mennonites no longer dress in plain clothing, nor are they collective.

Two groups of plain-dressing Mennonites still remain, both called Old Order. There are those who rely on a horse and buggy for transportation, like the Amish, and those who use motorized vehicles. The "horse-and-buggy Mennonites," as they are nicknamed, also speak Pennsylvania German, but they are distinguished from the Amish by their appearance. Mennonite men do not wear beards, and women are more likely to use fabrics with patterns or designs. They also hold church services in meeting houses, rather than homes, and use electricity from the grid. They prohibit the use of television and online services.

Amish

There are four primary groups that share the Amish name: Beachy Amish, Amish Mennonites, New Order, and Old Order. Both New Order and Old Order Amish rely on horse-and-buggy transportation, while Beachy Amish and Amish Mennonites are more relaxed in their use of technology. The horse-and-buggy Amish have numerous affiliations within these larger orders.

Related Groups

Still other religious groups have some theological affinity with the Amish but are not Anabaptist or "plain." Four groups—Friends ("Quakers"), Amana Colonies, Moravians, and Shakers—each have some similarity to the Amish in either beliefs or practices. This may include a historic effort to maintain a simple lifestyle, separation from the world, or an emphasis on nonresistance. None of these groups emerged from Anabaptist roots, nor do they have any direct historical or religious affiliation with the Amish. Of the four, the first three continue to attract members, but the Shakers are no longer in existence.

Notes

Preface

1. Those in a helping profession may perceive the decision to divulge this information as a violation of confidentiality. I am guided by the ethics of the American Psychological Association in situations such as these and believe I acted responsibly. In addition, for a discussion of the complexities that arise in the area of ethics and the Amish, see Cates, 2011.

2. Such global pronouncements are almost never true when speaking of the Amish. The statement is used here for dramatic effect, but in practice, few Amish church members join the National Rifle Association.

3. Johnson-Weiner, 2007.

4. Kraybill, Johnson-Weiner, and Nolt, 2013.

5. Weaver-Zercher, 2005.

6. Hostetler, 1992; Hostetler and Miller, 2005.

7. Sandahl, 2003.

8. Defined in the *Urban Dictionary*, www.urbandictionary.com.

9. There is a caveat to this statement, in that former Amish who identify as a sexual minority run LGBT Amish, https://www.lgbtamish.com, a website serving as "a network for lesbian, gay, bisexual, and transgender Amish and ex-Amish."

10. Wuthnow, 1989.

11. Foucault, 1978.

12. de Lauretis, 1991.

13. Graham, 2014, 6.

14. D. Hall, 2003.

15. Kraybill, 2001.

Chapter 1. The Pilgrim Journey

1. See Associated Press, 2018.

2. *Martyrs Mirror*, available in an English-language edition through the Herald Press, records the long history of persecution faced by those in the early church. Weaver-Zercher (2016) describes the history of this collection.

3. Kraybill, 2003, *Amish and the State*.

4. "Amish Population, 2018."

5. Kraybill, Johnson-Weiner, and Nolt, 2013.

6. See, for example, Curtin, Ventura, and Martinez, 2014.

7. Nolt (2015) has written a readable and thorough history of the Amish.

8. Hostetler, 1993.

9. See "Amish Population Change, 1992–2018."

10. Kraybill, Johnson-Weiner, and Nolt, 2013.

11. Foster (1997) compares and contrasts Amish and non-Amish cultures.

12. Kraybill, 1994.

13. Nolt, 2015.

14. See, for example, Olshan and Schmidt (1994) for a discussion of these rules and Amish women.

15. Kraybill, Johnson-Weiner, and Nolt, 2013, 118–119.

16. For an in-depth description of Amish religion and spirituality, see Kraybill, Nolt, and Weaver-Zercher (2010).

17. The Amish normally quote from the King James version (KJV) of the Bible. In deference to their practice, I do so as well throughout this book.

18. Kraybill, Johnson-Weiner, and Nolt, 2013, 162–165.

19. Stevick, 2014.

20. "Timely" varies by settlement. In some, Rumspringa may last for less than a year. In others, it may continue into a person's early twenties.

21. Kraybill, Johnson-Weiner, and Nolt, 2013, 78.

22. Kraybill, Johnson-Weiner, and Nolt, 2013, 88–90.

23. The exception proves the rule. See the case of Samuel Mullet, as reported by Kraybill (2014).

24. "Amish Population, 2018."

25. Kraybill, Johnson-Weiner, and Nolt, 2013, 203.

26. Hostetler (1993) has largely been outdated by more-recent research on and histories of the Amish, but his description of a church service (his chapter 10) remains an excellent overview.

27. Nolt, 2016, 47–48.

28. See Hostetler (1993, 77–83) for a description of the service of baptism.

29. Nolt, 2015.

30. Kraybill, 2010. See the entry for "Amish."

31. Kraybill, 2003, "Negotiating with Caesar."

32. Yoder, 2003.

33. McConnell and Hurst, 2006.

34. Hostetler, 1970.

35. For essays on various conflicts with the state in the twentieth century, consult Kraybill (2003, *Amish and the State*). Johnson-Weiner (2007) offers a history and comparison of Amish private schools in various communities.

36. Zook, 2003.

37. Olshan (1990) traces the development and functions of the Amish National Steering Committee.

38. Olshan, 1990.
39. Kraybill and Nolt, 2004.
40. Hostetler 1993, 234–251.
41. E. Hall, 1976.

Chapter 2. Peculiar People, Queer Theory

1. Toumey, 2010.
2. McKenzie, 2010.
3. See, for example, Burge, 2007; Chevrette, 2013; Offman, 2014.
4. Gamson and Moon, 2004.
5. Cragun and Sumerau, 2015.
6. Hartman, 2017.
7. de Souza, Brewis, and Rumens, 2016.
8. See, for example, Carr, Hagai, and Zurbriggen, 2017; Pettit, 2012.
9. Foucault, 1978; 1985; 1986.
10. Foucault, 1978, 17–49.
11. de Lauretis, 1991; Spargo, 1999.
12. Sullivan, 2003, "Social Construction of Same-Sex Desire."
13. Foucault, 1978, 27.
14. Foucault, 1985, 143–184.
15. Foucault, 1978, 103–114.
16. Loughlin, 2015.
17. Foucault, 1978.
18. Berger and Luckmann, 1967; de Lauretis and Schehr, 1991; Nagoshi, Hohn, and Nagoshi, 2017; Reynolds, 2017.
19. See, for example, Ruffolo, 2018; Sullivan, 2003, 189–206.
20. Berlant and Warner, 1998.
21. Bollen, 2002.
22. Pettit and Hegarty, 2014; Rosario and Scrimshaw, 2014.
23. Alexander and Yescavage, 2009.
24. Sullivan, 2003, 50–52.
25. Bailey, 1988; Kraybill, Johnson-Weiner, and Nolt, 2013, 64–66.
26. Stein and Plummer, 1994.
27. Cheng, 2015.
28. Stein and Plummer, 1994, 182.
29. Halperin, 1995.
30. Rubin, 2011.
31. *Family Life*, 2019; *Young Companion*, 2019.
32. Sedgwick, 1990.
33. Butler, 1999.
34. Thomas, 2009.
35. Sullivan, 2003.

36. Cheng, 2015; Sullivan, 2003.

37. Berlant and Warner, 1995.

38. Harry Chapin, "Cat's in the Cradle," 1974, from the album *Verities and Balderdash*.

39. The emphasis on plain dress has become even greater. See, for example, Anderson and Anderson, 2019.

40. Schrock-Shenk, 2007.

41. Kraybill, Johnson-Weiner, and Nolt, 2013, chapter 11.

Chapter 3. The Birds and the Bees (and the Horses and the Cows)

1. *Seinfeld*, "The Mango" episode.

2. T. S. Eliot, "The Hollow Men," cited in Ricks and McCue, 2015, 81.

3. Foucault, 1978, 10–12.

4. Some scholars who attend public schools may be exposed to sex education.

5. Johnson-Weiner, 2007.

6. Bender, 1930.

7. Bender, 1930, 144.

8. Kraybill, Johnson-Weiner, and Nolt, 2013, 346–347.

9. See Kraybill, 2001, 302–305.

10. Knust, 2011.

11. Kraybill and Nolt, 2004.

12. This reference is borrowed from the poem "High Flight," by John Gillespie Magee Jr.

13. Huntington, 1994.

14. Jim Europe's 369th Infantry Band, "How Ya Gonna Keep 'Em Down on the Farm (after They've Seen Paree?)," 1919, Pathé Records.

15. Keim, 2003.

16. Stevick, 2014, 275–298.

17. Vandenbosch and van Oosten, 2017.

Chapter 4. "Knowing" One Another

1. The term "knowing" as a euphemism for sexual behavior is taken from Genesis 4:1, KJV: "And Adam knew Eve his wife; and she conceived and bore Cain, and said, 'I have gotten a man from the Lord.'"

2. Kraybill, Johnson-Weiner, and Nolt, 2013, 69.

3. Laqueur, 2003.

4. Nolt, 2015, 353.

5. *Young Companion*, July 2014, 7.

6. *Young Companion*, July 2014, 14.

7. Robbins et al., 2011.

8. The biblical injunctions against masturbation are beyond the scope of this work, but the most frequently cited text is Genesis 38:9–10, KJV. It states

that Onan practiced coitus interruptus, ejaculating on the ground rather than impregnating his sister-in-law. The act displeased God and resulted in Onan's divine execution.

9. There are some cases of persons who do seek entry, however. See, for example, Anderson, 2016.

10. Some do consider the Amish to be a cult and work hard to challenge its presence. See, for example, the Mission to Amish People website, www .mapministry.org. With the exception of breakaway outlier groups, however, the Amish are not viewed as cult-like (Kraybill, 2014).

11. Nolt, 2016, 6.

12. Nolt, 2016, 6.

13. Faulkner, 2017.

14. Louden, 2016.

15. Cates, 2014, 3.

16. See Kraybill, Johnson-Weiner, and Nolt, 2013, 92–96.

17. Labrecque and Whisman, 2017.

18. The primary drug of choice, after alcohol, is marijuana, although other drugs are becoming increasingly common. For a discussion, see Cates and Weber, 2013.

19. Stevick, 2014.

20. Kraybill, Johnson-Weiner, and Nolt, 2013, 217–221.

21. Reiling (2002) does not specifically address this issue, but her description of females' perceptions of the Rumspringa period makes a poignant statement about their vulnerability.

22. This is the vestige of the Amish practice of bundling, occasionally still mentioned but rarely practiced.

23. Bailey, 1988.

24. Miller et al., 2007.

25. Kraybill, Johnson-Weiner, and Nolt, 2013, 158–159.

26. Hamilton, Martin, Osterman, and Rossen, 2019.

27. Marcotte, 2015.

28. Kriebel, 2007. This practice has also been called *Brauche*, or *Braucherei*. See Hostetler, 1976.

29. Zegers-Hochschild et al., 2009.

30. Not that community births always end well. See Rowe, 2012.

31. Meyers and Nolt, 2005, 132–135.

Chapter 5. Gender Roles

1. Cates, 2017. And be thankful the Amish don't fly. Imagine the crowds waiting for a family member to deplane at the airport!

2. Wittmer, 2010.

3. Johnson-Weiner, 2007, 235.

4. In some settlements, a few teachers will have obtained a General Equivalency Diploma (GED) or High School Equivalency (HSE) diploma, but this is rare.

5. Johnson-Weiner, 2007.

6. Kraybill, Johnson-Weiner, and Nolt, 2013, 214.

7. Reiling, 2002.

8. Stevick, 2014.

9. The author has observed females in English clothes, but they are more likely to be discrete in where and how they wear this apparel. And every statement about the Amish has a caveat. I vividly recall a summer in which I repeatedly observed a young Amish woman defiantly mowing her parent's lawn in a pair of "Daisy Dukes" (very short cutoff shorts), with a prayer covering firmly in place.

10. Cates, 2014, 146.

11. Bailey, 1988.

12. This assertion doubtless could make at least some readers cringe at the chauvinistic attitude it portrays. The current debates in mainstream culture remind us that these attitudes still have a pervasive influence.

13. Kraybill, Johnson-Weiner, and Nolt, 2013, 214.

14. Hostetler, 1993, 224–227.

15. Stevick, 2014.

16. Amish periodicals, such as *Family Life*, outline the practical expectations of a marriage, which are equally as important as love, trust, and communication to make the relationship work.

17. At times I have heard this ability, that is, ferreting out more information than needed about any individual, called "Amish Google."

18. Kraybill, Johnson-Weiner, and Nolt, 2013.

19. Johnson-Weiner, 2020.

20. Cheek and Piercy, 2004.

21. Kraybill, 2001; Kraybill and Nolt, 2004.

22. Wilcox, 2004.

23. Steven M. Nolt, personal communication, July 26, 2018.

24. Johnson-Weiner, 2001.

25. Miller et al., 2007.

Chapter 6. Intimacy

1. Rokach, 2007.

2. Wilson, 2016

3. Kraybill, 2010, 93.

4. Kline, 2017.

5. Hostetler, 1993, 5.

6. Kraybill, Johnson-Weiner, and Nolt, 2013, 65.

7. Kraybill, Johnson-Weiner, and Nolt, 2013, 100.

8. Nolt, 2016.

9. Rokach, 2007.

10. Seepersad, Choi, and Shin, 2008.

11. Multiple theorists have discussed this process. Piaget's model is well described in a book edited by Gruber and Vonèche, 1995.

12. One of the more open memoirs to demonstrate this struggle from a psychological perspective is Wagler, 2011.

13. Stevick, 2014, 221–222.

14. Stevick, 2014, 221–222.

15. Kraybill, 2008.

16. Kraybill, 2010, 7–10.

17. Hostetler, 1993, 284–299.

18. Mahoney and Cano, 2014.

19. Hernandez, Mahoney, and Pargament, 2011.

20. Kusner, Mahoney, Pargament, and DeMaris, 2014.

21. Rusu, Beach, Hilpert, and Turliuc, 2015.

22. Pollard, Riggs, and Hook, 2014.

23. This quote is attributed to Charles Dickens's novel *Barnaby Rudge*.

24. Savani, Mead, Stillman, and Vohs, 2016.

25. One group of Amish women established themselves as "The Sewing Circle" and published a booklet to support wives struggling with domestic violence. *The Doorway to Hope: For the Hurting, Struggled, and Discouraged* is available through amazon.com.

26. Kraybill, Johnson-Weiner, and Nolt, 2013, 68.

27. E. Carter, 2012.

28. Kraybill, Nolt, and Weaver-Zercher, 2010, 42–44.

29. For a discussion of the problems these types of relationship create, see Mackall, 2007.

30. See, for example, Gingrich and Lightman, 2004.

Chapter 7. Suffer Little Children

1. Kraybill, Nolt, and Weaver-Zercher, 2007.

2. Matthew 19:14.

3. See, for example, Finnerty 2017; Waterman, 2018.

4. Tolin and Foa, 2006.

5. Martinez-Catena, Redondo, Frerich, and Beech, 2017.

6. Chu and Thomas, 2010.

7. Seto, 2012.

8. See b4uact, www.b4uact.org, an online support group for individuals who prefer to remain abstinent from their desire for sexual activity with underage partners.

9. Jennings and Deming, 2017.

10. Mann, Hanson, and Thornton, 2010.

11. See, for example, McGuigan and Stephenson, 2015.

12. Gavey and Senn, 2014.

13. Lang and Frenzel, 1988.

14. U.S. Department of Justice, NSOPW, 2017.

15. Kraybill, 2001, 131–35.

16. A longstanding program is described in Cates, 2014, "Social Work and Social Services." It was detailed again by Boyer and Hoover, 2019. This program demonstrates exemplary teamwork between the state and the Amish, differing markedly from the challenges described here.

17. Ellis, 1951; Ellis, 1954. Now considered one of the foreparents of cognitive psychology, Ellis minimized the trauma of sexual assault and parsed blame onto women for their attitudes and morals when the crime did occur.

18. Letter from an Indiana bishop to an Adams County, Indiana, Department of Child Services Family Case Manager, February 2009.

19. McGuire and Miranda, 2008; Peck, 2015.

20. Boas, 1889; Rapport, 2014.

21. After an early session at their home, I walked out of the house to find all four of my car doors open. The young man apologized, explaining that his two youngest sisters, still of preschool age, were to blame. A car had never been parked that long at their farm before.

22. This is an indictment from one who has worked within the system. I have testified as an expert for both prosecutors and defense attorneys in non-Amish cases of sexual offenses, as well as completed numerous forensic psychological assessments for victims of sexual abuse and persons accused of sexual offenses.

23. These two undated and anonymous publications are synonymous across much of their material. *A Fence or An Ambulance?* is apparently the first to have been published, shortly after 2000, by a deacon and a minister in the Aylmer, Ontario, settlement.

24. See, for example, *Strong Families, Safe Children: An Amish Family Resource Book*. Pathway Publishers, in Aylmer, Ontario, has published this booklet since 2002, but it originated in the 1990s from a consortium of social service agencies in Ohio. Pathway distributed 9000 copies in the first five years of its publication.

25. See, for example, Fisher 2009, regarding the case of four Amish bishops charged with failure to report child abuse in Missouri. The story of this perceived injustice on the part of the civil authorities reverberated throughout Amish settlements.

Chapter 8. Victorian's Secret

1. Excerpted from a story in *Healing from Sexual Sin*, n.d.

2. A female reader who critiqued the manuscript for this book commented

that the current chapter was heavily weighted toward males, a valid complaint. My case studies and reports of Amish female experiences with paraphilias are more limited and less reliably reported; therefore I am reluctant to include them here.

3. American Psychiatric Association, 2013, 685.

4. Akins, 2004.

5. Gordon, 2008.

6. Moser, 2010.

7. Bhugra, Popelyuk, and McMullen, 2010.

8. McManus, Hargreaves, Rainbow, and Alison, 2013.

9. Sorrentino, 2017.

10. For a description of this program, see Weber, Cates, and Carey, 2010.

11. "Hastily assembled post-session dialogue" is a polite description for frantically grabbing my Amish co-leader as soon as the boys had left and asking, "What just happened in there!?"

12. Kraybill, 2001.

13. See Denko, 1976.

14. Charlton, 1997.

15. See Langevin, 2013, chapter 11.

16. The possibility of other victims who did not choose to come forward always exists in such cases.

17. Rowland, Cempel, and Tempel, 2018.

18. Kraybill, 2001.

Chapter 9. The Love That Won't Shut Up

1. The letter, including this section from it, is in the author's files.

2. Robertson Davies was a Canadian novelist, playwright, critic, journalist, and professor. While this saying has been attributed to him multiple times, the context was unavailable.

3. These changing attitudes are sampled in the "U.S. Religious Landscape Study," 2014.

4. A Pew Research poll found that 61% of Americans support gay marriage, while 31% oppose it. The sample was taken between March 20 and 25, 2019, and consisted of 1,503 adults. See "Majority of Public Favors," 2019.

5. For an example of the arguments for disassembling such monuments, see Staples, 2018.

6. "Queer community" is used here in lieu of "gay" or "G/L/B/T/Q" designations to encompass the variety of sexual minorities that now reside under the umbrella of nontraditional sexual preferences and gender statuses.

7. D. Carter, 2010; *American Experience*, 2019.

8. Olshan, 2003.

9. Federman, 2015.

10. Humphreys, 2008. His book has gone through several editions.

11. *Obergefell v. Hodges*, 2015, Supreme Court of the United States blog, www.scotusblog.com/casefiles/cases/obergefell-v-hodges.

12. See the LGBT Amish website, https://www.lgbtamish.com.

13. See the Mission to Amish People website, www.mapministry.org.

14. See, for example, Brewer, 2018, for a comparison of how rural men handle same-sex interests.

15. Mallory, Brown, and Conron, 2018.

16. Gonsiorek and Rudolph, 1991.

17. Shidlo, Schroeder, and Drescher, 2001.

18. In the United States, the number of persons identifying as lesbian, gay, bisexual, and transgender (LGBT) is rising. A 2012 Gallup poll found 3.5% identifying as one of these sexual minorities. By 2017, that number had risen to 4.5%. See Newport, 2018.

19. Sherry, Adelman, Whilde, and Quick, 2010.

20. Jennings, 2015.

21. The author has notes from interviews and conversations with Amish living in differing locales across the three largest settlements that include references to fondling, mutual masturbation, and oral sex at this age.

22. Meeus, Iedema, and Vollebergh, 1999.

23. D'Augelli, 2006.

24. Brown, 1998.

25. Stevick, 2014.

26. Cates, 2017, 113–116.

27. See Humphreys, 2008.

28. See, for example, Schwartz, 2014.

29. Herek, 2015.

30. Kraybill, 2003, *Amish and the State.*

Epilogue. Rubbing Shoulders with Rahab

1. The Amish reference their Rumspringa-age youth who step away from the rules of the community as stepping onto the "devil's playground."

2. Joshua 2:1–21, KJV.

3. Matthew 1:5, KJV.

4. Kraybill and Bowman, 2001, 259.

5. See Longenecker, 2018, for a recent essay on the subject.

6. Johnson-Weiner, 2020.

7. Johnson-Weiner, 2001.

8. Bailey, 1988.

9. Kraybill, Johnson-Weiner, and Nolt, 2013, 194.

10. I recall the first time an Amish minister from an extremely conservative

Amish church asked me to phone him. He owned a cell phone, he told me, but only used it on his construction job.

11. See, for example, Jantzi, 2017.

12. Weaver-Zercher, 2016.

13. See, for example, Primack et al., 2017.

14. Levenson, 2005.

15. Letter of resignation from Mary Beth Bonaventura, director, Indiana Department of Child Services, to Governor Eric Holcomb, December 12, 2017. Retrieved from DocumentCloud, https://www.documentcloud.org/documents/4332901-DCS-Director-Mary-Beth-Bonaventura-s-resignation.html.

16. Hostetler and Miller, 2005.

17. Cong, 1992.

Bibliography

Akins, Chana K. 2004. "The Role of Pavlovian Conditioning in Sexual Behavior: A Comparative Analysis of Human and Nonhuman Animals." *International Journal of Comparative Psychology*, 17(2), https://escholarship.org/uc/item/1wc177zt/.

Alexander, Jonathan, and Karen Yescavage. 2009. "'The Scholars Formerly Known as . . .': Bisexuality, Queerness, and Identity Politics." In *The Ashgate Research Companion to Queer Theory*, ed. Noreen Giffney and Michael O'Rourke, chapter 3. New York: Routledge.

American Experience. 2019. "Stonewall Uprising: The Year That Changed America." PBS, aired June 11.

American Psychiatric Association. 2013. *Diagnostic and Statistical Manual of Mental Disorders*, fifth edition. Washington, DC: American Psychiatric Association.

"Amish Population, 2018." Young Center for Anabaptist and Pietist Studies, Elizabethtown College, https://groups.etown.edu/amishstudies/statistics/population-2018/.

"Amish Population Change, 1992–2018." Young Center for Anabaptist and Pietist Studies, Elizabethtown College, https://groups.etown.edu/amishstudies/files/2018/08/Population_Change_1992-2018.pdf.

Anderson, Cory. 2016. "Religious Seeker's Attraction to the Plain Mennonites and Amish." *Review of Religious Research*, 58, 125–147.

Anderson, Cory, and Jennifer Anderson. 2019. *Fitted to Holiness: How Modesty Is Achieved and Compromised among the Plain People*. Millersburg, OH: Acorn Press.

Associated Press. 2018. "2 Adams County Amish Woman Get Probation in Midwifery Case," *U.S. News & World Report*, August 24, https://www.usnews.com/news/best-states/indiana/articles/2018-08-24/2-adams-county-amish-woman-get-probation-in-midwifery-case/.

Bailey, Beth L. 1988. *From Front Porch to Back Seat: Courtship in Twentieth-Century America*. Baltimore: Johns Hopkins University Press.

Bender, Harold S. 1930. "An Amish Church Discipline of 1781." *Mennonite Quarterly Review*, 4, 140–148.

Berger, Peter L., and Thomas Luckmann. 1967. *The Social Construction of Reality*. New York: Penguin.

Berlant, Lauren, and Michael Warner. 1995. "Guest Column: What Does
    Queer Theory Teach Us about X?" *PMLA*, *10*(3), 343–349.
Berlant, Lauren, and Michael Warner. 1998. "Sex in Public." *Critical Inquiry*,
    24(2), 547–566.
Bhugra, Dinesh, Dmitri Popelyuk, and Isabel McMullen. 2010. "Paraphilias
    across Cultures: Contexts and Controversies." *Journal of Sex Research*,
    47(2–3), 242–256.
Boas, Franz. 1889. "On Alternating Sounds." *American Anthropologist*, 2(1),
    47–54.
Bollen, Kenneth A. 2002. "Latent Variables in Psychology and the Social Sci-
    ences." *Annual Review of Psychology*, 53, 605–634.
Boyer, Robin, and Allen Hoover. 2019. "Dealing with Abuse." Paper presented
    on June 7 at Health and Well-Being in Amish Society: A Multidisciplinary
    Conference. Young Center for Anabaptist and Pietist Studies, Elizabeth-
    town College, Elizabethtown, PA.
Brewer, Mick. 2018. "Good Ol' Country Boys Playin' on the Farm: Online
    Articulations of Rural Masculinity by Men Who Have Sex with Men."
    Sexuality & Culture, 22, 355–379.
Brown, Laura S. 1998. "Lesbian Identities." In *Lesbian, Gay, and Bisexual
    Identities in Families: Psychological Perspectives*, ed. Charlotte Patterson
    and Anthony R. D'Augelli, 3–23. New York: Oxford University Press.
Burge, Barb J. 2007. "Bending Gender, Ending Gender: Theoretical Founda-
    tions for Social Work Practice with the Transgender Community." *Social
    Work*, 52(3), 243–256.
Butler, Judith. 1999. *Gender Trouble: Feminism and Subversion of Identity*.
    New York: Routledge.
Carr, Brandon Balzer, Ella Ben Hagai, and Eileen L. Zurbriggen. 2017. "Queer-
    ing Bem: Theoretical Intersections between Sandra Bem's Scholarship and
    Queer Theory." *Sex Roles*, 76, 655–668.
Carter, David. 2010. *Stonewall: The Riots That Sparked the Gay Revolution*.
    New York: St. Martin Griffin.
Carter, Erik. 2012. "Four Views of Christian Spirituality." *Spectrum*, August
    24, https://spectrummagazine.org/article/erik-carter/2012/08/24
    /four-views-christian-spirituality/.
Cates, James A. 2011. "Of Course It's Confidential: Only the Community
    Knows; Mental Health Interventions with the Old Order Amish." In *Ethical
    Conundrums, Quandaries, and Predicaments in Mental Health Practice:
    A Casebook from the Files of Experts*, ed. W. Brad Johnson and Gerald P.
    Koocher, chapter 35. New York: Oxford University Press.
Cates, James A. 2014. *Serving the Amish: A Cultural Guide for Professionals*.
    Baltimore: Johns Hopkins University Press.

Cates, James A. 2017. *Love, Life, & Laughter: The Amish in Essays and Stories*. n.p.: Cates & Associates. Available from amazon.com.

Cates, James A., and Chris Weber. 2013. "An Alcohol and Drug Intervention with Old Order Amish Youth: Preliminary Results of Culturally Segregated Class Participation." *Journal of Groups in Addiction and Recovery*, 8(2), 112–128.

Charlton, Randolph S. 1997. "Treatment of Paraphilias." In *Treating Sexual Disorders*, ed. Randolph S. Charlton, general ed. Irvin Yalom, chapter 9. San Francisco: Jossey-Bass.

Cheek, Cheryl, and Kathleen W. Piercy. 2004. "Quilting as Age Identity Expression in Traditional Women." *International Journal of Aging and Human Development*, 59(4), 321–337.

Cheng, Patrick S. 2015. "Contributions from Queer Theory." In *The Oxford Handbook of Theology, Sexuality, and Gender*, ed. Adrian Thatcher, 241–254. Oxford, England: Oxford University Press.

Chevrette, Roberta. 2013. "Outing Heteronormativity in Interpersonal and Family Communications: Feminist Applications of Queer Theory 'Beyond the Sexy Streets.'" *Communication Theory*, 23, 170–190.

Chu, Chi Meng, and Stuart D. M. Thomas. 2010. "Adolescent Sexual Offenders: The Relations`1992. "Amish Factionalism and Technological Change: A Case Study of Kerosene Refrigerators and Conservatism." *Ethnology*, 31(3), 2015–2018.

Cragun, Ryan T., and J. Edward Sumerau. 2015. "The Last Bastion of Sexual and Gender Prejudice?: Sexualities, Race, Gender, Religiosity, and Spirituality in the Examination of Prejudice toward Sexual and Gender Minorities." *Journal of Sex Research*, 52(7), 821–834.

Curtin, Sally C., Stephanie J. Ventura, and Gladys M. Martinez. 2014. "Recent Decline in Nonmarital Childbearing in the United States." NCHS Data Brief No.162, August. National Center for Health Statistics, www.cdc.gov /nchs/data/databriefs/db162.pdf.

D'Augelli, Anthony R. 2006. "Developmental and Contextual Factors and Mental Health among Lesbian, Gay, and Bisexual Youth." In *Contemporary Perspective on Lesbian, Gay, and Bisexual Psychology: Sexual Orientation and Mental Health; Examining Identity and Development in Lesbian, Gay, and Bisexual People*, ed. Allen M. Omato and Howard S. Kurtzman, 37–52. Washington, DC: American Psychological Association.

Denko, Joanne D. 1976. "Klismaphilia: Amplification of the Erotic Enema Deviance." *American Journal of Psychotherapy*, 30(2), 236–255.

de Lauretis, Teresa. 1991. "Queer Theory: Lesbian and Gay Sexualities; An Introduction." *Differences: A Journal of Feminist Cultural Studies*, 3(2), iii–xviii.

de Lauretis, Teresa, and Lawrence R. Schehr. 1991. *Queer Theory: Lesbian and Gay Sexualities*. Bloomington: Indiana University Press.

de Souza, Eloisio Moulin, Jo Brewis, and Nick Rumens. 2016. "Gender, the Body and Organization Studies: Que(e)rying Empirical Research." *Gender, Work, and Organization*, 23(6), 600–613.

Ellis, Albert. 1951. *The Folklore of Sex*. Oxford, England: Charles Dani.

Ellis, Albert. 1954. "Psychosexual and Marital Problems." In *An Introduction to Clinical Psychology*, ed. L. A. Pennington and Irwin A. Berg, 264–283. New York: Ronald Press.

Family Life. 2019. Available from Pathway Publishers, 43632 CR 390, Bloomingdale, MI.

Faulkner, Carolyn. 2017. "Identity Change among Ethno-Religious Border Crossers: The Case of Former Amish." *Review of Religious Research*, 59, 449–470.

Federman, Lillian. 2015. *The Gay Revolution: The Story of the Struggle*. New York: Simon & Schuster.

Finnerty, Meagen. 2017. "Police: Amish Bishop Charged for Failing to Report Abuse." *Lancaster Online*, May 13, posted May 17 on the Amish America website, https://amishamerica.com/amish-bishop-charged-for-failing-to -report-abuse/.

Fisher, Maria Sudekum, for the Associated Press. 2009. "4 Amish Bishops Charged with Not Reporting Child Molester Who Was Shunned." *Minneapolis–St. Paul Star Tribune*, November 3.

Foster, Thomas W. 1997. "American Culture through Amish Eyes: Perspectives of an Anarchist Protest Movement." *Social Thought and Research*, 20(1), 89–108.

Foucault, Michel. 1978. *The History of Sexuality. Volume 1: An Introduction*, trans. Robert Hurley. New York: Random House.

Foucault, Michel. 1985. *The History of Sexuality. Volume 2: The Use of Pleasure*, trans. Robert Hurley. New York: Random House.

Foucault, Michel. 1986. *The History of Sexuality. Volume 3: The Care of the Self*, trans. Robert Hurley. New York: Random House.

Gamson, Joshua, and Dawne Moon. 2004. "The Sociology of Sexualities: Queer and Beyond." *Annual Review of Sociology*, 30, 47–64.

Gavey, Nicola, and Charlene Y. Senn. 2014. "Sexuality and Sexual Violence." In *APA Handbook of Sexuality and Psychology. Volume 1: Person-Based Approaches*, ed. Deborah L. Tolman and Lisa M. Diamond, chapter 12. Washington, DC: American Psychological Association.

Gingrich, Luann Good, and Ernie Lightman. 2004. "Mediating Communities and Cultures: A Case Study of Informal Helpers in an Old Order Mennonite Community." *Families in Society*, 85(4), 511–514.

Gonsiorek, John C., and James R. Rudolph. 1991. "Homosexual Identity:

Coming Out and Other Developmental Events." In *Homosexuality: Research Implications for Public Policy*, ed. John C. Gonsiorek and James D. Weinrich, 161–176. Newbury Park, CA: Sage.

Gordon, Harvey. 2008. "The Treatment of Paraphilias: An Historical Perspective." *Criminal Behavior and Mental Health*, *18*, 79–87.

Graham, Mark. 2014. *Anthropological Explorations in Queer Theory: Queer Interventions*. New York: Routledge.

Gruber, Howard E., and J. Jacques Vonèche, eds. 1995. *The Essential Piaget*. North Vale, NJ: Aronson.

Hall, Donald E. 2003. *Queer Theories*. New York: Palgrave MacMillan.

Hall, Edward T. 1976. *Beyond Culture*. New York: Anchor Books.

Halperin, David. 1995. *Saint Foucault: Towards a Gay Hagiography*. New York: Oxford University Press.

Hamilton, Brady E., Joyce A. Martin, Michelle J. K. Osterman, and Lauren M. Rossen. 2019. "Births: Provisional Data for 2018." Vital Statistics Rapid Release No. 7, May. National Center for Health Statistics, https://www.cdc.gov/nchs/data/vsrr/vsrr-007-508.pdf.

Hartman, Eric. 2017. "The Queer Utility of Narrative Case Studies for Clinical Social Work and Practice." *Clinical Social Work Journal*, *45*, 227–237.

Healing from Sexual Sin. n.d. Topeka, IN: Healing Journey.

Herek, Gregory M. 2015. "Beyond 'Homophobia': Thinking More Clearly about Stigma, Prejudice, and Sexual Orientation." *American Journal of Orthopsychiatry*, *88*(5), S29–S37.

Hernandez, Krystal M., Annette Mahoney, and Kenneth I. Pargament. 2011. "Sanctification of Sexuality: Implications for Newlyweds' Marital and Sexual Quality." *Journal of Family Psychology*, *25*(5), 775–780.

Hostetler, John A. 1970. "Socialization and Adaptation to Public Schooling: The Hutterian Brethren and the Old Order Amish." *Sociological Quarterly*, *11*(2), 194–205.

Hostetler, John A. 1976. "Folk Medicine and Sympathy Healing among the Amish." In *American Folk Medicine: A Symposium*, ed. Wayland D. Hand, 248–258. Los Angeles: University of California Press.

Hostetler, John A. 1992. "An Amish Beginning." *American Scholar*, *61*(4), 552–562.

Hostetler, John A. 1993. *Amish Society*, fourth edition. Baltimore: Johns Hopkins University Press.

Hostetler, John A., and Susan Fisher Miller. 2005. "An Amish Beginning." In *Writing the Amish: The Worlds of John A. Hostetler*, ed. David Weaver Zercher, 5–35. University Park: Pennsylvania State University Press.

Humphreys, Laud. 2008. *Tearoom Trade: Impersonal Sex in Public Places*, enlarged edition. New Brunswick, NJ: Aldine Transaction.

Huntington, Gertrude Enders. 1994. "Persistence and Change in Amish Education." In *The Amish Struggle with Modernity*, ed. Donald B. Kraybill and Marc A. Olshan, 77–95. Hanover, NH: University Press of New England.

Jantzi, Charles. 2017. "Amish Youth and Social Media: A Phase or a Fatal Error?" *Mennonite Quarterly Review*, 91(1), 71–80.

Jennings, Jerry L., and Adam Deming. 2017. "Review of the Empirical and Clinical Support for Group Therapy Specific to Sexual Abusers." *Sexual Abuse*, 29(8), 731–764.

Jennings, Theodore W., Jr. 2015. "Same-Sex Relations in the Biblical World." In *The Oxford Handbook of Theology, Sexuality, and Gender*, ed. Adrian Thatcher, chapter 13. New York: Oxford University Press.

Johnson-Weiner, Karen M. 2001. "The Role of Women in Old Order Amish, Beachy Amish, and Fellowship Churches." *Mennonite Quarterly Review*, 75(April), 231–256.

Johnson-Weiner, Karen M. 2007. *Train Up a Child: Old Order Amish and Mennonite Schools*. Baltimore: Johns Hopkins University Press.

Johnson-Weiner, Karen M. 2020. *The Lives of Amish Women*. Baltimore: Johns Hopkins University Press.

Keim, Albert N. 2003. "Military Service and Conscription." In *The Amish and the State*, second edition, ed. Donald B. Kraybill, 43–64. Baltimore: Johns Hopkins University Press.

Kline, Paul A. 2017. "Gelassenheit: A Bible Principle." *Family Life*, March, 7–9.

Knust, Jennifer Wright. 2011. *Unprotected Texts: The Bible's Surprising Contradictions about Sex and Desire*. New York: HarperCollins.

Kraybill, Donald B. 1994. "The Amish Encounter with Modernity." In *The Amish Struggle with Modernity*, ed. Donald B. Kraybill and Marc A. Olshan, chapter 2. Hanover, NH: University Press of New England.

Kraybill, Donald B. 2001. *The Riddle of Amish Culture*, revised edition. Baltimore: Johns Hopkins University Press.

Kraybill, Donald B. 2003. *The Amish and the State*, second edition. Baltimore: Johns Hopkins University Press.

Kraybill, Donald B. 2003. "Negotiating with Caesar." In *The Amish and the State*, second edition, ed. Donald B. Kraybill, chapter 1. Baltimore: Johns Hopkins University Press.

Kraybill, Donald B. 2008. "Amish Informants: Mediating Humility and Publicity." In *The Amish and the Media*, ed. Diane Zimmerman Umble and David Weaver-Zercher, chapter 7. Baltimore: Johns Hopkins University Press.

Kraybill, Donald B. 2010. *Concise Encyclopedia of Amish, Brethren, Hutterites, and Mennonites*. Baltimore: Johns Hopkins University Press.

Kraybill, Donald B. 2014. *Renegade Amish: Beard Cutting, Hate Crimes, and the Trial of the Bergholz Barbers*. Baltimore: Johns Hopkins University Press.

Kraybill, Donald B, and Carl Desportes Bowman. 2001. *On the Backroad to Heaven: Old Order Hutterites, Mennonites, Amish, and Brethren.* Baltimore: Johns Hopkins University Press.

Kraybill, Donald B., Karen M. Johnson-Weiner, and Steven M. Nolt. 2013. *The Amish.* Baltimore: Johns Hopkins University Press.

Kraybill, Donald B., and Steven M. Nolt. 2004. *Amish Enterprise: From Plows to Profits,* second edition. Baltimore: Johns Hopkins University Press.

Kraybill, Donald B., Steven M. Nolt, and David Weaver-Zercher. 2007. *Amish Grace: How Forgiveness Transcended Tragedy.* San Francisco: Jossey-Bass.

Kraybill, Donald B., Steven M. Nolt, and David Weaver-Zercher. 2010. *The Amish Way: Patient Faith in a Perilous World.* San Francisco: Jossey-Bass.

Kriebel, David W. 2007. *Powwowing among the Pennsylvania Dutch: A Traditional Medical Practice in the Modern World.* University Park: Pennsylvania State University Press.

Kusner, Katherine G., Annette Mahoney, Kenneth I. Pargament, and Alfred DeMaris. 2014. "Sanctification of Marriage and Spiritual Intimacy Predicting Observed Marital Interactions across the Transition to Parenthood." *Journal of Family Psychology,* 28(5), 604–614.

Labrecque, Lindsay T., and Mark A. Whisman. 2017. "Attitudes toward and Prevalence of Extramarital Sex and Descriptions of Extramarital Partners in the 21st Century." *Journal of Family Psychology,* 31(7), 952–957.

Lang, Reuben A., and Roy R. Frenzel. 1988. "How Sex Offenders Lure Children." *Annals of Sex Research,* 1, 303–317.

Langevin, Ron. 2013. "Voyeurism." In *Sexual Strands: Understanding and Treating Sexual Anomalies,* chapter 11. New York: Routledge.

Laqueur, Thomas W. 2003. *Solitary Sex: A Cultural History of Masturbation.* New York: Zone Books.

Levenson, Jacob. 2005. *The Secret Epidemic: The Story of AIDS and Black America.* New York: Anchor Books.

Longenecker, Fr. Dwight. 2018. "Ireland and the End of Cultural Catholicism." *Catholic World Report,* May 28, https://www.catholicworldreport.com/2018/05/28/ireland-and-the-end-of-cultural-catholicism/.

Louden, Mark L. 2016. *Pennsylvania Dutch: The Story of an American Language.* Baltimore: Johns Hopkins University Press.

Loughlin, Gerard. 2015. "Gay Affections." In *The Oxford Handbook of Theology, Sexuality, and Gender,* ed. Adrian Thatcher, 608–623. Oxford, England: Oxford University Press.

Mackall, Joe. 2007. *Plain Secrets: An Outsider among the Amish.* Boston: Beacon Press.

Mahoney, Annette, and Annmarie Cano. 2014. "Introduction to the Special Section on Religion and Spirituality in Family Life: Delving into Relational Spirituality for Couples." *Journal of Family Psychology,* 28(5), 583–586.

"Majority of Public Favors Same-Sex Marriage, but Divisions Persist: Little Change in Opinion since 2017." 2019. Pew Research Center, May 14, https://www.people-press.org/2019/05/14/majority-of-public-favors -same-sex-marriage-but-divisions-persist/.

Mallory, Christy, Taylor N. T. Brown, and Kerith J. Conron. 2018. "Conversion Therapy and LGBT Youth." The Williams Institute, UCLA School of Law, January, https://williamsinstitute.law.ucla.edu/wp-content/uploads /Conversion-Therapy-LGBT-Youth-Jan-2018.pdf.

Mann, Ruth E., R. Karl Hanson, and David Thornton. 2010. "Assessing Risk for Sexual Recidivism: Some Proposals on the Nature of Psychologically Meaningful Risk Factors." *Sexual Abuse: A Journal of Research and Treatment*, 22(2), 191–217.

Marcotte, Amanda. 2015. "5 Ways Birth Control Has Changed America." *Rolling Stone*, June 6.

Martinez-Catina, Ana, Santiago Redondo, Nina Frerich, and Anthony R. Beech. 2017. "A Dynamic Risk Factors–Based Typology of Sexual Offenders." *International Journal of Offender Therapy and Comparative Criminology*, 61(14), 1623–1647.

McConnell, David L., and Charles E. Hurst. 2006. "No 'Rip Van Winkles' Here: Amish Education since *Wisconsin v. Yoder*." *Anthropology and Education Quarterly*, 37(3), 236–254.

McGuigan, William M., and Sarah J. Stephenson. 2015. "A Single-Case Study of Resiliency after Extreme Incest in an Old Order Amish Family." *Journal of Child Sexual Abuse*, 24, 526–537.

McGuire, Thomas G., and Jeanne Miranda. 2008. "New Evidence Regarding Racial and Ethnic Disparities in Mental Health: Policy Implications." *Health Affairs*, 27(2), 393–403.

McKenzie, Susan. 2010. "Genders and Sexualities in Individuation: Theoretical and Clinical Explorations." *Journal of Analytical Psychology*, 55, 91–111.

McManus, Michelle, Paul Hargreaves, Lee Rainbow, and Laurence J. Alison. 2013. "Paraphilias: Definition, Diagnosis, and Treatment." *F1000 Prime Reports*, 5, 36. doi: 10:127/P5–36.

Meeus, Wim H. J., Jurion Iedema, and Wilma A. M. Vollebergh. 1999. "Patterns of Adolescent Identity Development: Review of Literature and Longitudinal Analysis." *Developmental Review*, 19(4), 419–461.

Meyers, Thomas J., and Steven M. Nolt. 2005. *An Amish Patchwork: Indiana's Old Orders in the Modern World*. Bloomington, IN: Quarry Press.

Miller, Kirk, Berwood Yost, Sean Flaherty, Marianne Hillemeier, Gary Chase, Carol Weisman, and Anne Marie Dyer. 2007. "Health Status, Health Conditions, and Health Behaviors among Amish Women: Results from the Central Pennsylvania Women's Health Study (CePAWHS)." *Women's Health Issues*, 17, 162–171.

Moser, Charles. 2010. "Problems with Ascertainment." *Archives of Sexual Behavior*, 39, 1225–1227.

Nagoshi, Julie L., Kris L. Hohn, and Craig T. Nagoshi. 2017. "Questioning the Heteronormative Matrix: Transphobia, Intersectionality, and Gender Outlaws within the Gay and Lesbian Community." *Social Development Issues*, 39(3), 19–31.

Newport, Frank. 2018. "In U.S., Estimate of LGBT Population Rises to 4.5%." Gallup, https://news.gallup.com/poll/234863/estimate-lgbt-population-rises .aspx.

Nolt, Steven M. 2015. *A History of the Amish*, third edition. New York: Good Books.

Nolt, Steven M. 2016. *The Amish: A Concise Introduction*. Baltimore: Johns Hopkins University Press.

Offman, Hilary. 2014. "The Princess and the Penis: A Post-Modern Queer-y Tale." *Psychoanalytic Dialogues*, 24, 72–87.

Olshan, Marc A. 1990. "The Old Order Amish Steering Committee: A Case Study in Organizational Evolution." *Social Forces*, 69, 603–616.

Olshan, Marc. 2003. "The National Amish Steering Committee." In *The Amish and the State*, second edition, ed. Donald B. Kraybill, 67–84. Baltimore: Johns Hopkins University Press.

Olshan, Marc A., and Kimberly D. Schmidt. 1994. "Amish Women and the Feminist Conundrum." In *The Amish Struggle with Modernity*, ed. Donald B. Kraybill and Marc A. Olshan, chapter 13. Hanover, NH: University Press of New England.

Peck, Jennifer H. 2015. "Minority Perceptions of the Police: A State-of-the-Art Review." *Policing: An International Journal of Police Strategies and Management*, 38(1), 173–203.

Pettit, Michael. 2012. "The Queer Life of a Lab Rat." *History of Psychology*, 15(3), 212–227.

Pettit, Michael, and Peter Hegarty. 2014. "Psychology and Sexuality in Historical Time." In *APA Handbook of Sexuality and Psychology. Volume 1: Person-Based Approaches*, ed. Deborah L. Tolman and Lisa M. Diamond, 63–78. Washington, DC: American Psychological Association.

Pollard, Sara E., Shelley A. Riggs, and Joshua N. Hook. 2014. "Mutual Influences in Adult Romantic Attachment, Religious Coping, and Marital Adjustment." *Journal of Family Psychology*, 28(5), 615–624.

Primack, Brian A., Ariel Shensa, Jaime Sidani, Erin O. Whaite, Liu yi Lin, Daniel Rosen, Jason B. Colditz, Ana Radovic, and Elizabeth Miller. 2017. "Social Media Use and Perceived Isolation among Young Adults in the U.S." *American Journal of Preventive Medicine*, 53(1), 1–8.

Rapport, Nigel. 2014. *Social and Cultural Anthropology: The Key Concepts*, third edition. New York: Routledge.

Reiling, Denise M. 2002. "The 'Simmie' Side of Life: Old Order Amish Youths' Affective Response to Culturally Prescribed Deviance." *Youth and Society*, 34(2), 161–171.

Reynolds, Celene. 2017. "How Sexual Identities Change: Pragmatism, Habit, and Creativity in the 'Situation' of the Lascivious Costume Ball." *Qualitative Sociology*, 40, 215–235.

Ricks, Christopher, and Jim McCue. 2015. *The Poems of T. S. Eliot. Volume 1: Collected and Uncollected Poems.* Baltimore: Johns Hopkins University Press.

Robbins, Cynthia, Vanessa Schick, Michael Reece, Debra Herbenick, Stephanie A. Sanders, Brian Dodge, and J. Dennis Fortenberry. 2011. "Prevalence, Frequency, and Associations of Masturbation with Partnered Sexual Behaviors among US Adolescents." *Archives of Pediatric Medicine, 165*(12), 1087–1093. doi: 10.1001/dchpediatrics.2011.142.

Rokach, Ami. 2007. "The Effect of Age and Culture on the Causes of Loneliness." *Social Behavior and Personality*, 35(2), 169–186.

Rosario, Margaret, and Eric W. Scrimshaw. 2014. "Theories and Etiologies of Sexual Orientation." In *APA Handbook of Sexuality and Psychology. Volume 1: Person-Based Approaches*, ed. Deborah L. Tolman and Lisa M. Diamond, 555–596. Washington, DC: American Psychological Association.

Rowe, Rod. 2012. "Two Midwives Arrested on Felony Charges." *Goshen [IN] News*, April 4, https://www.goshennews.com/news/two-midwives-arrested-on-felony-charges/article_ce0988ab-cab8-5fbf-b574-7091be219d03.html.

Rowland, David L., Laura M. Cempel, and Aaron R. Tempel. 2018. "Women's Attributes Regarding Why They Have Difficulty Reaching Orgasm." *Journal of Sex & Marital Therapy*, 44(5), 1–10, https://doi.org/10.1080/009 2623x.2017.1408046/.

Rubin, Gayle. 2011. *Deviations: A Gayle Rubin Reader*. Durham, NC: Duke University Press.

Ruffolo, David V. 2018. "Post-Queer Considerations." In *The Ashgate Research Companion to Queer Theory*, ed. Noreen Giffney and Michael O'Rourke, chapter 22. New York: Routledge.

Rusu, Petruta P., Steven R. H. Beach, Peter Hilpert, and Maria N. Turliuc. 2015. "Dyadic Coping Mediates the Association of Sanctification with Marital Satisfaction and Well-Being." *Journal of Family Psychology*, 29(6), 843–849.

Sandahl, Carrie. 2003. "Queer Crips." *GLO: A Journal of Lesbian and Gay Studies*, 9(1–2), 25–56.

Savani, Krishna, Nicole L. Mead, Tyler Stillman, and Kathleen D. Vohs. 2016. "No Match for Money: Even in Intimate Relationships and Collectivist Cultures, Reminders of Money Weaken Sociomoral Responses." *Self and Identity*, 15(3), 342–355.

Schrock-Shenk, Carolyn. 2007. *Stumbling toward a Genuine Conversation on Homosexuality: Living Issues Discussion*, Series 4, 13–18. Telford, PA: Cascadia.

Schwartz, James. 2014. "The Amish Closet." August 6, LGBT Amish, https://
www.lgbtamish.com/news/the-amish-closet/.

Sedgwick, Eve Kosofsky. 1990. *Epistemology of the Closet*. Berkeley: University of California Press.

Seepersad, Sean, Mi-Kyung Choi, and Nana Shin. 2008. "How Does Culture Influence the Degree of Romantic Loneliness and Closeness?" *Journal of Psychology*, 142(2), 209–216.

Seto, Michael C. 2012. "Is Pedophilia a Sexual Orientation?" *Archives of Sexual Behavior*, 41 (1), 231–236.

Sherry, Alissa, Andrew Adelman, Margaret Whilde, and Daniel Quick. 2010. "Competing Selves: Negotiating the Intersection of Spiritual and Sexual Identities." *Professional Psychology: Research and Practice*, 41(2), 112–119.

Shidlo, Ariel, Michael Schroeder, and Jack Drescher, eds. 2001. *Sexual Conversion Therapy: Ethical, Clinical, and Research Perspectives*. New York: Haworth Medical Press.

Sorrentino, Renee. 2017. "DSM-5 and Paraphilias: What Psychiatrists Need to Know." Institute for Sexual Wellness, March 2, www.instituteforsexualwellness.org/dsm-5-and-paraphilias-what-psychiatrists-need-to-know/.

Spargo, Tomsin. 1999. *Foucault and Queer Theory*. New York: Totem Books.

Staples, Brent. 2018. "Monuments to White Supremacy," *New York Times*, January 9, https:www.nytimes.com/2018/01/09/opinion/monuments -white-supremacy-tennessee.html.

Stein, Arlene, and Ken Plummer. 1994. " 'I Can't Even Think Straight': 'Queer' Theory and the Missing Sexual Revolution in Sociology." *Sociological Theory*, 12(2), 178–187.

Stevick, Richard A. 2014. *Growing Up Amish: The Rumspringa Years*, second edition. Baltimore: Johns Hopkins University Press.

Sullivan, Nikki. 2003. *A Critical Introduction to Queer Theory*. New York: New York University Press.

Thomas, Calvin. 2009. "On Being Post-Normal: Heterosexuality after Queer Theory." In *The Ashgate Research Companion to Queer Theory*, ed. Noreen Giffney and Michael O'Rourke, chapter 1. New York: Routledge.

Tolin, David F., and Edna B. Foa. 2006. "Sex Differences in Trauma and Posttraumatic Stress Disorder: A Quantitative Review of 25 Years of Research." *Psychological Bulletin*, 132 (6), 959–992.

Toumey, Chris. 2010. "Elegance and Empiricism." *Nature and Nanotechnology*, 5, 693–694.

U.S. Department of Justice, Dru Sjodin National Sex Offender Public Website (NSOPW). 2017. "Raising Awareness About Sexual Abuse: Facts and Statistics."

"U.S. Religious Landscape Study." 2014. Pew Research Center, June 4–September 30, https://www.pewforum.org/dataset/pew-research-center-2014-u-s -religious-landscape-study/.

Vandenbosch, Laura, and Johanna F. M. van Oosten. 2017. "The Relationship between Online Pornography and the Sexual Objectification of Women: The Attenuating Role of Porn Literacy Education." *Journal of Communication*, 67(6), https://doi.org/10.1111/jcom.12341/.

Wagler, Ira. 2011. *Growing Up Amish*. Carol Stream, IL: Tyndale House.

Waterman, Cole. 2018. "Amish Man Faces 18 Counts of Sexual Assault Involving 3 Girls." 2018. *Bay City [MI] News*, August 14, https://www.mlive.com/news/bay-city/2018/08/amish_man_faces_18_counts_of_s.html.

Weaver-Zercher, David L. 2005. *Writing the Amish: The Worlds of John A. Hostetler*. University Park: Pennsylvania State University Press.

Weaver-Zercher, David L. 2016. *Martyrs Mirror: A Social History*. Baltimore: Johns Hopkins University Press.

Weber, Chris, James A. Cates, and Shirley Carey. 2010. "A Drug and Alcohol Intervention with Old Order Amish Youth: Dancing on the Devil's Playground." *Journal of Groups in Addiction and Recovery*, 5, 97–112.

Wilcox, W. Bradford. 2004. "New Fathers: Religion, Ideology, and Fatherhood." In *Soft Patriarchs, New Men: How Christianity Shapes Fathers and Husbands*, chapter 4. Chicago: University of Chicago Press.

Wilson, Ara. 2016. "The Infrastructure of Intimacy." *Signs: Journal of Women in Culture and Society*, 41(2), 247–280.

Wittmer, Joe. 2010. *The Gentle People: An Inside View of Amish Life*, fourth edition. n.p.: WittmerBooks@Bellsouth.net.

Wuthnow, Robert. 1989. *Meaning and Moral Order: Explanations in Cultural Analysis*. Berkeley: University of California Press.

Yoder, Paton. 2003. "The Amish View of the State." In *The Amish and the State*, second edition, ed. Donald B. Kraybill, chapter 2. Baltimore: Johns Hopkins University Press.

Young Companion, July 2014, 7 and 14. Available from Pathway Publishers, 43632 CR 390, Bloomingdale, MI.

Young Companion. 2019. Available from Pathway Publishers, 43632 CR 390, Bloomingdale, MI.

Zegers-Hochschild, F, G. O. Adamson, J. de Mouzon, O. Ishihara, R. Mansour, K. Nygren, E. Sullivan, and S. van der Poel, on behalf of ICMART and WHO. 2009. "The International Committee for Monitoring Assisted Reproductive Technology (ICMART) and the World Health Organization (WHO) Revised Glossary on ART Terminology, 2009." *Human Reproduction*, 24(11), 2683–2687.

Zook, Lee J. 2003. "Slow-moving Vehicles." In *The Amish and the State*, second edition, ed. Donald B. Kraybill, chapter 8. Baltimore: Johns Hopkins University Press.

Index

7, 27, 41, 55, 71, 75, 91, 92, 93, 94, 95,
116, 128, 142, 143, 145, 162, 167, 168;
and intimacy, 90, 91–92, 93–105, 148;
and lack of privacy, 56–57; marriage in,
84, 100, 135; and online communication, 50–51; and paraphilias, 128–34,
136–37; and queer theory, 26–27; and
spirituality, 156–57; support by, 42
confession, 11, 61, 104, 159; and child
abuse, 113, 114, 119; for deviance, 29,
46, 51; and healing, 60; and homosexuality, 144; humiliation of, 113, 131;
and masturbation, 52, 55, 56; and
paraphilias, 127–28, 131, 133, 134; and
Rumspringa, 62, 83; variations in, 8,
59–60; voluntary vs. requested, 113.
See also church
Congress, 13
conscientious objectors, 49, 141, 154
constructionism, 21–22, 24, 30, 47
contraception, 64–66, 67, 157
coprolalia, 133–34, 136
courts/justice system, 1–2, 24, 107, 131,
167. *See also* civil authorities/government;
law/legal system
cows and bulls game, 19–20, 22–23, 28,
147–48, 150
critical thinking, x, xi–xii, 41, 48
cross-dressing, 34, 125, 130
cultural relativism, 118, 126

Dahmer, Jeffrey, 162
Dangerfield, Rodney, 52
dating, 31, 63, 64, 79, 80, 81, 84
Davies, Robertson, 140, 181n2
dawdyhaus, 32, 33, 87, 98
deacons, viii, 9, 10, 32, 35, 85. *See also*
clergy
deviance, x, xii, 29–30, 46, 51, 61,
125–26, 128, 131, 143
discipleship, 58, 91
divorce, 5, 41, 42, 62, 70, 99, 100, 168.
See also marital separation
drag queens, 141
drug use, xi, 62, 63, 79, 81, 177n18. *See
also* alcohol use
dyspareunia (painful intercourse), 129

education, viii, 5, 13, 17, 31, 39–40, 50,
57, 76–78. *See also* knowledge; schools

elderly people, 32, 33, 87–88, 89, 98
electricity, 5, 17, 50, 56
Elkhart-LaGrange settlement, xiii, 59, 80
erectile dysfunction, 129
evangelism, 7, 101
excommunication, 3, 8–9, 11, 60, 95, 102,
103, 107, 133, 163. *See also* shunning
exhibitionism, 125

families, 10, 49, 56, 63, 69, 80, 87–88, 89,
153, 158; and child abuse, 112–13; and
childcare, 74–75; and collective culture,
34, 97; extended, 9, 31, 32, 74–75, 85,
97, 100, 149; gender roles in, 9, 33, 34,
35–36, 74–75, 78, 84; and homosexuality, 144, 145; intimacy in, 104, 167;
and marriage, 85, 99, 100, 149; and
Rumspringa, 8, 57; size of, 65–66, 74.
See also children; fathers; mothers;
parents; siblings
Family Life, 28, 54, 178n16
fathers, 9, 34, 35–36, 52, 86, 98, 106–7,
111, 112, 149, 163. *See also* husbands;
men; parents
Fellowship churches, 157
feminism, 22, 25, 27, 73, 157, 159. *See
also* women
Fence or an Ambulance, A?, 120
finances, 11, 13, 40, 44, 57, 73, 84, 85, 86,
97, 119, 157, 160
foot fetish, 124, 145
foreplay, 46, 130, 135, 136
forgiveness, 9, 60, 62, 64, 102, 103, 133,
134; and child abuse, 106–8, 113,
114–15, 119, 121, 159. *See also* sin
Foucault, Michel, xi, 22, 38; *The History
of Sexuality*, 23–24
Friends (Quakers), 172
friends/friendships, 8, 11, 43, 56, 58, 67,
80; and cell phones, 158; and child
abuse, 111; and collective, high-context
culture, 84; and gender roles, 31; and
intimacy, 92, 93, 94, 99, 103, 104;
and lifespan, 31; and marriage, 70;
non-Amish, 103, 104; with persons
in mainstream culture, 103; and
Rumspringa, 8; and schooling, 76; and
sexual minorities, 145, 150–51, 152,
162, 168; support from, 42
frottage, 46

teachers/teaching, viii, 76–77, 78, 178n4. *See also* education; schools
technology, 14–16, 17, 44, 49, 50–51, 65, 146, 157, 170, 172; and different affiliations, 12; disagreements over, 163; and education, 5; and Hutterites, 171; and Mennonites, 171; and Ordnung, 5, 128; physical work ethic vs., 48; reproductive, 67; and social change, 16. *See also* cell phones
telephone scatologia, 125
Toumey, Chris, 21
Tower of Babel, 38
transgender persons, vii, ix, x, 25, 74, 130, 142, 146, 152, 162, 164
Troyer, 12
trust, 71, 95, 96, 148–49

Unfriddah, 59, 104, 134
urophilia, 125

vaginismus, 129
Victoria, Queen, 124
voyeurism, 35, 125, 132–33, 136

Walk in the Light, 120–21
Wilcox, W. Bradford, 86
Wisconsin v. Yoder et al., 13
wives, 70; authority of, 100; and chastity, 81; and child abuse, 107; and domestic violence, 99–100, 179n25; gender roles of, 73, 84, 86, 87, 88, 157; and home, 44; and identity, 29; lifetime commitment to, 62; and marital dissatisfaction, 41–42; and menstruation, 40; and pleasure, 46; sex as restricted to, viii; and sexual minorities, 149; as struggling,

41, 42, 70; submission by, viii, 32. *See also* marriage; women
women, ix, 1–2, 16, 44, 87, 97, 147, 158–59; authority of, 32, 36, 76–77, 78, 86–87, 100, 135; and business, 10, 86; and child abuse, 111; and clergy, 10, 11; and clothing, 17, 178n9; empowerment of, 66, 81; and Foucault, 22; gender roles of, 28–29, 31, 36, 72, 73, 84, 86–87, 88, 157, 162; as healthcare professionals, 74; and hierarchical culture, 110, 111; as homemakers, 31–32, 44, 78, 86; and marriage proposals, 84; as matriarchs, 34, 36, 37, 84, 88; and menstruation, 40; and Ordnung, 84; and paraphilias, 135, 180–81n2; and patriarchy, 10; and pleasure, 37–38; and pregnancy termination, 168; and Rumspringa, 62, 63, 79, 81, 157; as single, 42, 157; and soft patriarchy, 86, 88, 157; subjugation of, 100, 104; submission by, viii, 4, 10, 28–29, 31–32, 36, 63, 67, 74, 77, 84, 86, 87, 88, 104, 135, 146, 157, 158; as teachers, 76–77, 78; vocations and avocations of, 84; and work, 44, 77, 86. *See also* feminism; girls; lesbians; midwives; mothers; wives
work, 32, 43–45, 48, 70, 77, 81, 86, 158
World War I, 49

Young Companion, 28; "The Battle Leading Up," 55; "A Way to Escape," 54–55
youth, 54, 56; and Rumspringa, vii, 8, 57, 62–63, 78–82; tenuous values of, 158–59. *See also* adolescents; children

zoophilia, 51, 120, 127–28, 146